Storage
Virtualization

Storage Virtualization

Technologies for Simplifying Data Storage and Management

Tom Clark

✦ Addison-Wesley

Upper Saddle River, NJ • Boston• Indianapolis • San Francisco
New York • Toronto • Montreal • London • Munich • Paris
Madrid • Capetown • Sydney • Tokyo • Singapore • Mexico City

The publisher offers excellent discounts on this book when ordered in quantity for bulk purchases or special sales, which may include electronic versions and/or custom covers and content particular to your business, training goals, marketing focus, and branding interests. For more information, please contact:

U. S. Corporate and Government Sales
(800) 382-3419
corpsales@pearsontechgroup.com

For sales outside the U. S., please contact:

International Sales
international@pearsoned.com

Visit us on the Web: www.awprofessional.com

Library of Congress Catalog Number:
2004116051

ISBN 0-32-126251-4
Text printed in the United States on recycled paper at R. R. Donnelley, Crawfordsville, Indiana.
First printing, March 2005

This book is
dedicated to
the anonymous men and women
whose labor, from the
silicon foundries, factories and assembly lines
scattered around the globe,
brings advanced technologies
from the realm of ideas
to practical and productive
implementation

Contents

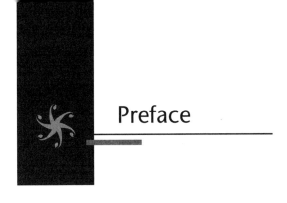

Preface

THE FOLLOWING WORK provides an overview of storage virtualization technology and its myriad manifestations. Like any emerging technical trend, the vague outlines of virtual storage concepts have only begun to sharpen as the technology has matured to productive applications in the real world. Today, there is a diversity of storage virtualization solutions, often tailored to meet specific storage needs. This book attempts to explain the background for that diversity, how different solutions function, and the essential value that is driving storage virtualization towards higher levels of utility.

Chapter 1 (Introduction), discusses the current state of storage virtualization in the market, and provides core concepts for understanding the hierarchy of virtualization-enabled storage operations.

The following three chapters provide foundation knowledge for understanding the relationship between what the user sees and what is done behind the scenes. Chapter 2 (Files and Records) begins with data in its more familiar format, as objects manipulated by applications for persistent storage. Chapter 3 (Data on Disk) provides the link between upper layer file/record structures and lower layer block data storage. Ultimately, all data must reside somewhere, and at some point the content of a file or record will be transformed into data blocks. Chapter 4 (The Storage Interconnect) reviews the connectivity required to link servers with their storage assets, whether by direct-attached SCSI, Fibre Channel or iSCSI.

The next five chapters discuss storage virtualization proper and the various means that have been engineered to support it. Chapter 5 (Abstracting Physical Storage) examines the process of aggregating multiple storage systems into a virtual storage pool. The secret recipe behind this is the mapping of logical block addresses presented by each system to virtual block addresses that are in turn presented to servers. This may be done in various ways. Chapter 6 (Virtualization at the Host) discusses software virtualization that runs on individual servers. Chapter 7 (Virtualization at the Storage Target) discusses array-based virtualization techniques that are offered in some form by nearly all storage vendors. Chapter 8 (Fabric-based Virtualization) reviews the integration of virtualization technology with fabric switches and initiatives such as the Fabric Application Interface Standard that promise interoperable solutions. Chapter 9 (Virtualization Appliances) examines fabric-attached solutions and the innies/outties dispute between in-band and out-of-band methods. Collectively, these chapters address the "where it is done" category of the SNIA storage virtualization taxonomy.

Chapter 10 (Virtualization Services) discusses the practical application of virtual storage to real problems such as high availability and heterogeneous storage use. Storage virtualization in general is a foundation for higher level storage services such as hierarchical storage management.

Chapter 11 (Virtualized SAN File Systems) reviews another use of virtualization technology to streamline file system management and to enable distributed computing environments.

Chapter 12 (Virtualized Tape) provides an overview of the application of virtualization and system aggregation concepts to classic tape backup operations. New technologies such as RAIT (Redundant Array of Independent Tape devices) are breathing new life into an established fixture of data center environments.

Chapter 13 (Storage Automation and Virtualization) discusses the higher level services that are enabled by storage virtualization. Policy-based storage management, application-sensitive virtualization intelligence and the ability of applications themselves to leverage underlying virtualized services are new areas of development that hold great promise for simplifying storage operations.

In conclusion, Chapter 14 (The Storage Utility) examines the wide range of technical dependencies that have been setting the pace of development of storage virtualization technology. As is typical for a final chapter, Chapter 14 also provides wild speculations on the future of storage virtualization and the benefits it may yet provide as an enabling technology for a storage utility.

I have included a bibliography, which unfortunately seems to be an endangered species in technical works these days. Although there are few works on storage virtualization, there are many fine references on SAN technology that the serious reader can pursue. There is also a glossary of storage virtualization terminology as well as general SAN concepts.

The Appendix section at the end of the book includes additional reference material that hopefully will be of interest. Appendix A (Industry Resources) provides web links to industry and standards organizations. Appendix B (Vendor Resources) provides web links to storage virtualization and storage networking vendors, grouped by product type. Appendix C (Observations & Speculations) is an opportunity for industry observers, analysts, experts and customers to express their opinions on what this technology is and where it might be going.

Intended Audience

The following work should be useful for anyone who wants to understand the higher functions of storage networking. Storage managers, administrators, SAN architects, storage engineers, analysts, vendors, students and anyone involved in data storage technology should appreciate the new opportunities that storage virtualization provides. This book is therefore intended for a fairly diverse audience, from readers who already have experience with SANs to those who are just learning the benefits of shared storage solutions.

It is always difficult, however, to write a technical work with a specific reader in mind. Some readers will want more technical content; others less. Some will appreciate a broader overview, while others will want to get immediately to the point. This book attempts to provide both sufficient technical detail to be meaningful for a technical audience, and sufficient overview to provide an understanding of the subject by a less technical reader. For both types of readers, feel free to fast forward through sections that discuss concepts already well-understood, or simply of less interest.

Throughout the text I have attempted to avoid mention of specific products or vendors. This is done both to preserve objectivity in discussing technical matters as well as to extend the useful shelf life of the work despite the inevitable innovations that will be introduced. Hopefully, the concepts and relationships explained in the following chapters will provide a useful framework for understanding where we are in the space-time continuum of virtualization's maturation into more sophisticated products.

Acknowledgments

TECHNOLOGY IS A COLLECTIVE ENTERPRISE, both within companies and among the companies that comprise an industry. I have had the good fortune of meeting and working with hundreds of technologists, engineers, system architects and administrators in the storage networking industry over the past eight years. In that time, networked storage has evolved into a successful mainstream technology and transformed data storage processes. Although market competition sometimes throws the storage family into dysfunction, the industry as a whole continues to spawn new solutions and new companies while attracting new talent to further technical innovation. The embodiment of the shared storage family is the Storage Networking Industry Association (SNIA), which should be credited for its contributions to standards, interoperability, education and technology advancement, and for bringing order from the chaos of vendor conflict. In the area of storage virtualization specifically, the SNIA has helped to clarify concepts and relationships within a still emerging and often confusing subject area.

Publishing is also a very collective effort. From the initial idea for a book to its appearance on a shelf, a work passes through many hands. For a technical work in particular, peer review is required to ensure technical accuracy and objectivity of content. I would like to thank Steve Blumenau, Mark Carlson, Milan Merhar and David Thiel for subjecting themselves to the review of the manuscript and for their many useful suggestions and observations. I also am indebted to Mary Franz and Catherine Nolan, my editors, and Lori Lyons, Noreen Regina and many others at Addison Wesley for overseeing this project and accommodating my sporadic output due to my heavy travel schedule.

As always, my wife Lou bears the brunt of personal sacrifice that accompanies a writing project. Although she does not share my interest in logical block address mapping algorithms, she understands that this is something I will probably outgrow at some point. In the meantime, she patiently waits for me to emerge from my study, back into multi-faceted reality to share a stroll through the garden or perhaps to help spread another ton of compose on it.

Due to my position at McDATA Corporation, I've traveled extensively over the past year, meeting customers and technologists throughout the US as well as Europe, Australia, New Zealand, India and Asia. My thanks to the many users of storage networking technology for their profound insight into the challenges of aligning technology to diverse application requirements and for affirming the global value of a technology that still has far more to offer in the future.

Tom Clark
Seattle, Washington

About the Author

TOM CLARK has held director positions at McDATA Corporation and other storage networking companies, conducts SAN seminars and tutorials worldwide, and serves as customer liaison. A noted storage industry author and advocate, he is a former board member of the Storage Networking Industry Association (SNIA) and has held chair positions for SNIA customer initiatives and the SNIA Interoperability Committee. His previous Addison-Wesley books include *Designing Storage Area Networks, Second Edition* (ISBN 0321136500) and *IP SANs: A Guide to iSCSI, iFCP, and FCIP Protocols for Storage Area Networks* (ISBN 0201752778). Tom lives in scenic Duvall, WA.

1 Introduction

1.1 Storage Virtualization Overview

The **data storage industry** is one of the most dynamic sectors in information technology today. Due largely to the introduction of high-performance networking between servers and storage assets, storage technology has undergone a rapid transformation as one innovation after another has pushed storage solutions forward. At the same time, the viability of new storage technologies is repeatedly affirmed by the rapid adoption of networked storage by virtually every large enterprise and institution. Businesses, governments, and institutions today depend on information, and information in its unrefined form as data ultimately resides somewhere on storage media. Applying new technologies to safeguard this essential data, facilitate its access, and simplify its management has readily understandable value.

Since the early 1990s, storage innovation has produced a steady stream of new technology solutions, including Fibre Channel, network-attached storage (NAS), server clustering, serverless backup, high-availability dual-pathing, point-in-time data copy (snapshots), shared tape access, storage over distance, iSCSI, CIM (common information model)-based management of storage assets and transports, and storage virtualization. Each of these successive waves of technical advance has been accompanied by disruption to previous practices, vendor contention, over-hyping of what the new solution could actually do, and confusion among customers. Ultimately, however, each step in technical development eventually settles on some useful application, and all the marketing dust finally settles back into place.

No storage networking innovation has caused more confusion in today's market, however, than storage virtualization. In brief, storage virtualization is the *logical abstraction of physical storage systems* and thus, when well implemented, hides the complexity of physical storage devices and their specific requirements from management view. Storage virtualization has tremendous potential for simplifying storage administration and reducing costs for managing diverse storage assets.

Unlike previous new protocols or architectures, however, storage virtualization has no standard measure defined by a reputable organization such as INCITS (InterNational Committee for Information Technology Standards) or the IETF (Internet Engineering Task Force). The closest vendor-neutral attempt to make storage virtualization concepts comprehensible has been the work of the Storage Networking Industry Association (SNIA), which has produced useful tutorial content on the various flavors of virtualization technology. Still, storage virtualization continues to play the role of elephant to the long lines of vendors and customers who, having been blinded by exaggerated marketing claims, attempt to lay hands on it in total darkness. Everyone walks away with a different impression. It is often difficult, therefore, to say exactly what the technology is or should be expected to do.

As might be expected, some of the confusion over storage virtualization is vendor-induced. Storage virtualization products vary considerably, as do their implementation methods. Vendors of storage arrays may host virtualization directly on the storage controller, while software vendors may port virtualization applications to servers or SAN appliances. Fabric switch manufacturers may implement virtualization services within the fabric in the form of smart switch technology. Some vendors implement storage virtualization commands and data along the same path between server and storage, while others split the control path and data path apart. Advocates of one or the other virtualization method typically have sound reasons why their individual approach is best, while their competitors are ever willing to explain in even greater detail why it is not. The diversity of storage virtualization approaches alone forces customers into a much longer decision and acquisition cycle as they attempt to sort out the benefits and demerits of the various offerings and try to separate marketing hype from useful fact.

In addition, it is difficult to read data sheets or marketing collateral on virtualization products without encountering extended discussions about point-in-time data copying via snapshots, data replication, mirroring, remote extension over IP, and other utilities. Although storage virtualization facilitates these services, none are fundamentally dependent on storage virtualization technologies. The admixture of core storage virtualization concepts such as storage pooling with ancillary concepts such as snapshots contributes to the confusion over what the technology really does.

Although storage virtualization technology has spawned new companies and products, virtualizing storage is not new. Even in open systems environments, atomic forms of virtual storage have been around for years. In 1987, for example, researchers Patterson, Gibson, and Katz at the University of California Berkeley published a document entitled "A Case for Redundant Arrays of Inexpensive Disks (RAID)," which described means to combine multiple disks and virtualize them to the operating system as a single large disk. Although RAID technology was intended to enhance storage performance and provide data recoverability against disk failure, it also streamlined storage management by reducing disk administration from many physical objects to a single virtual one. Today, storage virtualization technologies leverage lower-level virtualizing techniques such as RAID, but primarily focus on virtualizing higher-level storage systems and storage processes instead of discrete disk components.

The economic drivers for storage virtualization are very straightforward: reduce costs without sacrificing data integrity or performance. Computer systems in general are highly complex, too complex, in fact, to be administered at a discrete physical level. As computer technology has evolved, a higher proportion of CPU cycle time has been dedicated to abstracting the underlying hardware, memory management, input/output, and processor requirements from the user interface. Today, a computer user does not have to be conversant in assembly language programming to make a change in a spreadsheet. The interface and management of the underlying technology has been heavily virtualized.

Storage administration, by contrast, is still tedious, manual-intensive, and seemingly never-ending. The introduction of storage networking has centralized storage administrative tasks by consolidating dispersed direct-attached storage assets into larger, shared resources on a SAN. Fewer administrators can now manage more disk capacity and support more servers, but capacity for each server must still be monitored, logical units manually created and assigned, zones established and exported, and new storage assets manually brought online to service new application requirements. In addition, although shared storage represents a major technological advance over direct-attached storage, it has introduced its own complexity in terms of implementation and support. Complexity equates to cost. Finding ways to hide complexity, automate tedious tasks, streamline administration, and still satisfy the requirements of high performance and data availability saves money, and that is always the bottom line. That is the promise of storage virtualization, although many solutions today are still far short of this goal.

Another highly advertised objective for storage virtualization is to overcome vendor interoperability issues. Storage array manufacturers comply with the appropriate SCSI and Fibre Channel standards for basic connectivity to their products. Each, however, also implements proprietary value-added utilities and features to differentiate their offerings to the market and these, in turn, pose interoperability problems for customers with heterogeneous storage environments. Disk-to-disk data replication solutions, for example, are vendor-specific: EMC's version only works with EMC; IBM's only with IBM. By virtualizing vendor-specific storage into its vanilla flavor, storage virtualization products can be used to provide data replication across vendor lines. In addition, it becomes possible to replicate data from higher-end storage arrays with much cheaper disk assets such as JBODs (just a bunch of disks), thus addressing both interoperability and economic issues.

The concept of a system level storage virtualization strategy occurs repeatedly in vendor collateral. One of the early articles was Compaq's Enterprise Network Storage Architecture and its description of a *storage utility*. According to the ENSA document, this technology would transform storage ". . . into a utility service that is accessed reliably and transparently by users, and is professionally managed with tools and technology behind the scenes. This is achieved by incorporating physical disks into a large consolidated pool, and then virtualizing application disks from the pool."

The operative words here are *reliably* and *transparently*. Technical remedies, like doctors, must first do no harm. Reliability implies that storage data is highly accessible, protected, and at expected performance of delivery. Transparency implies that the complexity of storage systems has been successfully masked from view and that tedious administrative tasks have been automated on the back end. The abstraction layer of storage virtualization therefore bears the heavy burden of preserving the performance and data integrity requirements of physical storage while reducing the intricate associations between physical systems to a simple utility outlet into which applications can be plugged. Part of the challenge is to get the abstraction apparition conjured into place; a greater challenge is to ensure that the mirage does not dissolve when unexpected events or failures occur in the physical world. Utilities, after all, are expected to provide continuous service regardless of demand. You shouldn't have to phone the power company every time you wish to turn on a light.

The notion of utility applied to storage and compute resources conveys not only reliability and transparency, but also ubiquity. The simpler a technology becomes, the more widely it may be deployed. Storage networking is still an esoteric technology and requires expertise to design, implement and support. The substantial research, standards requirement definition, product development, testing, certification, and interoperability required to create operational SANs was in effect funded by large enterprise customers who had the most pressing need and budget to support new and complex storage solutions. Once a storage networking industry was established, however, shared storage expanded beyond the top tier enterprises into mainstream businesses. Leveraging storage virtualization to create a storage utility model will accelerate the market penetration of SANs and, in combination with other technologies such as iSCSI, spread shared storage solutions to small and medium businesses as well.

Currently, all major storage providers have some sort of storage virtualization strategy in place, with varying degrees of implementation in products. Upon acquiring Compaq, Hewlett-Packard (HP) inherited the ENSA (and ENSA-2) storage utility white paper and has supplemented it with its Storage Grid and other initiatives. IBM has TotalStorage with SAN Volume Controller. EMC's Information Lifecycle Management (ILM) extends storage virtualization's reach throughout the creation and eventual demise of data. Hitachi Data Systems supports array-based storage virtualization on its 9000 series systems. Even Sun Microsystems has a component for pooling of storage resources within its N1 system virtualization architecture. These vendor-driven storage virtualization initiatives reflect both proactive and reactive responses to the customers' desire for simplified storage management and are being executed through both in-house development and acquisition of innovative startups.

In addition, multilateral partnerships are being forged between vendors of virtualization software, storage providers, SAN switch manufacturers, and even nonstorage vendors such as Microsoft to bring new storage virtualization solutions to market. Despite the high confusion factor (and often contributing to it), storage virtualization development has considerable momentum and continues to spawn a diversity of product offerings. This is typical of an evolutionary process, with initial variation of attributes, cross-pollination, inheritance of successful features, and ultimately a natural selection for the most viable within specific environments. Because storage virtualization is still evolving, it is premature to say which method will ultimately prevail. It is likely that storage virtualization will continue to adapt to a diversity of customer environments and appear in a number of different forms in the storage ecosystem.

1.2 Core Concepts

The SNIA taxonomy for storage virtualization is divided into three basic categories: what is being virtualized, where the virtualization occurs, and how it is implemented. As illustrated in Figure 1.1, virtualization can be applied to a diversity of storage categories.

What is being virtualized may include disks (cylinder, head, and sector virtualized into logical block addresses), blocks (logical blocks from disparate storage systems may be pooled into a common asset), tape systems (tape drives and tape systems may be virtualized into a single tape entity, or subdivided into multiple virtual entities), file systems (entire file systems may be virtualized into shared file systems), and file or record virtualization (files or records may be virtualized on different volumes). Where virtualization occurs may be on the host, in storage arrays, or in the network via in-

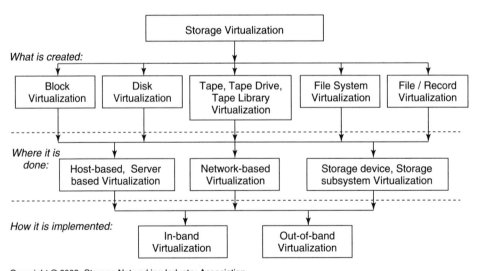

Figure 1.1 The SNIA storage virtualization taxonomy separates the objects of virtualization from location and means of execution.

telligent fabric switches or SAN-attached appliances. How the virtualizaton occurs may be via in-band or out-of-band separation of control and data paths. While the taxonomy reflects the complexity of the subject matter, the common denominator of the various whats, wheres, and hows is that storage virtualization provides the means to build higher-level storage services that mask the complexity of all underlying components and enable automation of data storage operations.

The ultimate goal of storage virtualization should be to simplify storage administration. This can be achieved by a layered approach, binding multiple levels of technologies on a foundation of *logical abstraction*. Concealing the complexity of physical storage assets by only revealing a simplified logical view of storage is only a first step towards streamlining storage management. Treating multiple physical disks or arrays as a single logical entity segregates the user of storage capacity from the physical characteristics of disk assets, including physical location and unique requirements of the physical devices. Storage capacity for individual servers, however, must still be configured, assigned, and monitored by someone. Although one layer of complexity has been addressed, the logical abstraction of physical storage alone does not lift the burden of tedious manual administration from the shoulders of storage managers.

To fulfill its promise, storage virtualization requires *automation* of the routine soul-numbing tasks currently performed by storage administrators. Allocating additional storage capacity to a server, for example, or increasing total storage capacity by introducing a new array to the SAN are routine and recurring tasks begging for automation.

Ideally, storage automation should be *policy-based* to further reduce manual intervention. Virtualization intelligence should automatically determine whether a specific storage transaction warrants high availability storage or less expensive storage, requires immediate data replication off-site or simple backup to tape on a predetermined schedule, or becomes part of a lifecycle management mechanism and retired at the appropriate time. A tiered infrastructure leveraging *class of storage* provides policy engines with repositories that meet the requirements of different types of storage transactions.

Finally, storage virtualization should become *application-aware*, so that policy-based automation responds to specific data types and identifies the unique needs of each upper layer application. Digital video, for example, gains more consistent performance if it is written to the outer, longer tracks of physical disks. Likewise, financial transactions for banking or e-commerce would benefit from frequent point-in-time copy policies for safeguarding most current transactions. An intelligent entity within the storage network that monitors and identifies applications and, based on preset policies, automates the handling of data for class of storage brings storage virtualization much closer to the concept of utility.

Application-aware storage virtualization provides the potential for dynamic communication between upper-layer applications and the storage services beneath them. As demonstrated by Microsoft's initiative to provide enhanced interfaces between the operating system and storage utilities such as snapshot, mirroring, and multi-pathing, it will become possible for upper layer applications to more fully leverage underlying storage services. *Storage virtualization-enabled applications* could, for example, seek out those services that more closely align to their current requirements for capacity or class of storage or, via APIs, inform the storage network of unique policies that should be enforced.

The viability of storage virtualization is enhanced by, but not dependent on, *interoperability* between storage assets. Although storage virtualization vendors highlight the benefits their products bring to heterogeneous data centers that may include HP, IBM, EMC, HDS, or other storage, some customers are quite happy with single vendor, homogeneous storage solutions. Logical abstraction of physical storage, automation of tedious tasks, policy-driven data handling, and application awareness have significant value for both single-vendor and multivendor storage networks. Interoperability, however, is a key component of the storage utility, since a utility should accommodate any type of application, operating system, computer platform, SAN infrastructure, storage array, or tape subsystem without manual intervention.

As shown in Figure 1.2, storage virtualization technology is a layered parfait of more sophisticated functionality that drives toward greater degrees of simplicity. Current products provide bits and pieces of a virtualized solution, from elementary storage pooling to limited automation and policy engines. Vendors and customers, however, are still struggling toward more comprehensive, utility-like storage virtualization strategies that fully leverage the potential of the technology.

Where the intelligence to do all these virtual things resides is interesting from a technical standpoint, but of less interest to the ultimate consumers of storage resources. The transparency that storage virtualization provides for storage assets should eventually apply to the storage virtualization solution

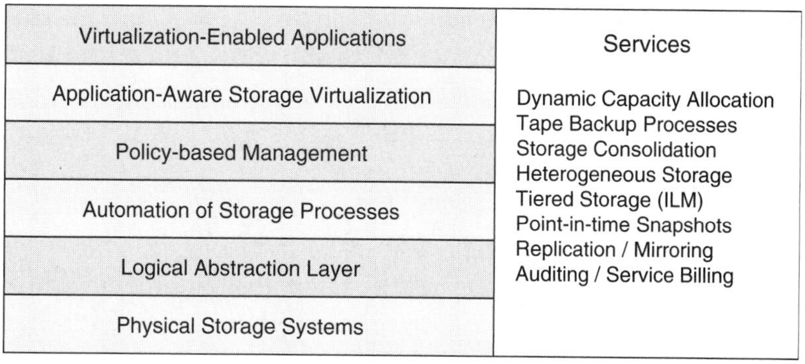

Virtualization-Enabled Applications	Services
Application-Aware Storage Virtualization	Dynamic Capacity Allocation
	Tape Backup Processes
Policy-based Management	Storage Consolidation
	Heterogeneous Storage
Automation of Storage Processes	Tiered Storage (ILM)
	Point-in-time Snapshots
Logical Abstraction Layer	Replication / Mirroring
	Auditing / Service Billing
Physical Storage Systems	

Figure 1.2 Storage virtualization enables successive layers of advanced functionality to fully automate storage administration.

itself. The abstraction layer that masks physical from logical storage may reside on host systems such as servers, within the storage network in the form of a virtualization appliance, as an integral option within the SAN interconnect in the form of intelligent SAN switches, or on storage array or tape subsystem targets. In common usage, these alternatives are referred to as *host-based*, *network-based*, or *array-based* virtualization. Each approach has strengths and weaknesses that we will describe in subsequent chapters.

In addition to differences between where virtualization intelligence is located, vendors have different methods for implementing virtualized storage transport. The *in-band* method places the virtualization engine squarely in the data path, so that both block data and the control information that govern its virtual appearance transit the same link. The *out-of-band* method provides separate paths for data and control, presenting an image of virtual storage to the host by one link and allowing the host to directly retrieve data blocks from physical storage on another. In-band and out-of-band virtualization techniques are sometimes referred to as symmetrical and asymmetrical, respectively, but for the sake of accuracy and simplifying the virtualization vocabulary, this text uses the hyphenated band terminology.

Simplifying storage administration through virtualization technology has many aspects. Centralizing management, streamlining tape backup processes, consolidating storage assets, enhancing capacity utilization, facilitating data integrity via snapshots, and so on, are not really attributes of storage virtualization, but rather beneficiaries of it. Storage consolidation, for example, is enabled by networking storage assets in a SAN. If there is only one large disk array to manage, virtualization may not contribute significantly to ease of use. If there are multiple disk arrays, and in particular, arrays from different vendors in the SAN, storage virtualization can help streamline management by aggregating the storage assets into a common pool. Current vendor literature is often punctuated with exclamations about the many benefits of storage virtualization, and then proceeds to focus on backup, snapshots, and so on. In some cases, customers may indeed benefit from these enhanced utilities, but may not need to virtualize anything to use them. As always, the starting point for assessing the potential benefit of a new technology is to understand your application requirements and your existing practices and measure potential benefit against real need.

In the following chapters, we will examine the basic problems that storage virtualization is trying to solve, the different approaches technologists are proposing, and the intersections between current capabilities and productive use by customers. In the process, hopefully, the confusion factor generated by this subject can be kept to a minimum as the virtual state of this technology is separated from its real one.

1.3 Chapter Summary

Storage Virtualization Overview

- Storage virtualization depends upon lower layer standards but is not defined by a standards body.

- Storage virtualization provides an abstraction layer over physical storage systems and enables multiple storage assets to be treated as a single logical entity.

- Granular forms of storage virtualization occur in technologies such as RAID.

- The value of storage virtualization is in its ability to automate tedious administrative tasks and reduce costs of storage management.

- The Compaq ENSA initiative leverages storage virtualization for creation of a storage utility.

- Storage virtualization must maintain reliable and transparent access to underlying storage assets.

- Virtualization technology is being driven by all major storage providers.

Core Concepts

- Virtualization provides a foundation of logical abstraction upon which more advanced functionality can be built.

- To streamline storage operations, logical abstraction should support automation of routine administrative tasks.

- Automated processes should be policy-based to further reduce manual intervention.

- Logical abstraction, automation, and policy-driven management enable storage virtualization to support application-aware storage management.

- The tight integration of operating systems and virtualization technology will enable applications to more fully leverage virtualized storage.

- Storage virtualization facilitates interoperability of storage systems.

- Virtualization technology can be supported on hosts, networks, or storage arrays and tape subsystems.

- In-band virtualization provides both control and data along the same connection path.

- Out-of-band virtualization separates control and data on different connection paths.

- Not all storage environments require or benefit from virtualization.

2

Files and Records

APPLICATIONS ARE USED TO create and manipulate user data to produce meaningful results. Data resides in transitory form in computer memory and in persistent form as data blocks on disk or tape. This chapter reviews the intermediate organization of data into files or records, depending on the requirements of upper layer applications.

2.1 Application Access to Data

Data in IT environments is information that has been converted to a machine-readable, digital binary format. Information in the form of data is the raw material for application processing, transport, and management. User data is input and digitized, manipulated, and then served up in intelligible, human readable form.

Data is the passive object of various types of active controlling mechanisms, which in turn may be defined by unique control-specific data points required for manipulation by applications. An IP datagram, for example, is composed of the data payload of useful information, and the packet header contains bits of control data required for proper transport of the payload from source to destination. In conventional usage, control data is often referred to as *control information*, with the generic term *data* reserved for the useful information that is the object of computer manipulation. The separation of control and data is fundamental to data processing and appears in various forms throughout information technology, including data placement on storage and the virtualization of storage assets.

Familiar applications such as word processing, email, and spreadsheet programs operate on discrete units of data in the form of files or records. In addition to the user-generated content within a file, the application will format the data with specific attributes appropriate for displaying the data within that application. A Microsoft Word file, for example, will contain the user content with the relevant paragraph, bolding, and font markers, as well as embedded attributes required for formatting by Word itself. This typically makes the file unreadable by another word processing program without a file conversion utility to strip Word-specific attributes and translate Word format markers into corresponding markers for the new application. Applications thus impose their own specific formatting requirements on user content, infusing user data with unique control bits for content manipulation and presentation.

The files and records that we access via applications are containers of user content. A file is a named string of contiguous data bytes that is stored persistently on disk or some other storage media. With appropriate access permissions, contiguous groups of bytes within a file may be read or modified, as well as extended by additional bytes. A record differs somewhat from a file in that its contents are highly structured, as for example, a group of data fields that is part of a medical patient information database. Multiple records can be assembled into a file or stored separately as distinct data sets of records. A file by contrast may be any type of digitized data, structured or unstructured, including binary code for computer instructions, compressed audio in MP3 format, numeric data for a financial spreadsheet, or the graphical and text content of yet another unsolicited email.

Whether an application accesses data as files or records, the application itself is also simply a collection of files, pulled sequentially into computer memory for execution. Compared to the potentially volatile nature of user data files that may be created, modified, or deleted at will, the files that contain application executables are relatively static. Once installed, these files rarely change unless the application version is upgraded or the application is removed. Depending on the operating system, an application's executable files may be dispersed throughout a file system hierarchy, with file dependencies embedded in the executable or referenced though a separate file. Dynamic link libraries (DLLs), for example, may reside alongside operating system executables and an application's main executables called from a common application folder.

In addition to user content for applications and the applications themselves, files are used to service the operating system that hosts the applications that, in turn, process user data. Turn on a server or workstation and one file after another is read into memory and executed to boot the system, until all the files required to operate have been loaded. Operating system-specific files may have their own data files, specifying variable content such as the system registry in Windows. In the end, all the executable code required for system operation, the variable parameters, auxiliary information, applications and their associated run-time data, and the end user data processed by those applications reside as files or records and are stored on disk.

2.2 Data as Files

The user-generated content and embedded application attributes compose the body of a file as it is manipulated by the application in computer memory. When the file is written to disk, however, additional information is associated with the file in the form of file *metadata*. File metadata provides control information on the file, including file attribute information such as file name, ownership, read/write permissions, system or application usage, date of last revision, and so on, depending on the specific requirements of the file system. Unlike application attributes that are embedded in user data, file metadata may be maintained and managed separately from the file's data content. This segregation facilitates file management and enables modification of the data with few changes to its metadata tracking information.

The metadata structure may vary from one file system to another. In the Unix File System (UFS), for example, the file metadata is defined by a 128 byte *inode* structure as follows:

Unix Inode

File type and access permissions

Number of links to this file

Owner ID number

Group ID number

Number of bytes in file

Time stamp for last file access

Time stamp for last file modification

Time stamp for last inode modification

Generation number

Number of extents (disk blocks that contain file data)

Version of inode

List of disk blocks for file data

Disk device containing blocks

For Unix, the file attributes listed by an inode structure may define both data files and file system directories, as well as physical storage devices that are treated as files. For data files, the inode structure typically does not contain actual file data, but provides pointers to where that data resides. Windows NTFS, by contrast, provides a file attribute record format that accommodates some file data (~1500 bytes) for fast retrieval of small files or directory entries. If the file data exceeds the capacity of the attribute record, pointers are provided to the first block of file content on disk. Windows NTFS file attributes include fields such as:

NTFS File Attributes

Time stamp and link count

Location of extended attributes beyond the current record

File name (up to 255 characters)

Security descriptor for ownership/access rights

File data

Object ID for distributed link tracking

Index root

Index allocation

Volume information

Volume name

File metadata is used by both the file system and upper layer applications to manage file creation, modification, access, and data placement. As new files are created and old ones moved or deleted, the associated inodes or file attribute records are also generated or deleted. Management of multiple files requires a separate application for management, and it is the role of a file system to oversee this process, using file metadata to monitor the life cycle of discrete files. Although the specific method of monitoring file metadata is operating system specific, common elements such as file naming, access permissions, time stamping, and data allocation are required to ensure proper tracking of files.

File metadata is control information about specific files within a particular file system structure (e.g., NTFS). The term metadata, however, is also used to describe other forms of control information. In storage virtualization terminology, metadata may refer to the mapping between virtual storage locations and real ones. In this text, control information for virtualizing storage assets is referred to as *storage metadata*, to differentiate it from the more granular file metadata.

2.2.1 File Naming Conventions

For most file systems, the file name can be up to 255 characters long. Windows NTFS (New Technology File System) and Unix, for example, support long file names and do not require a file extension identifier (e.g., *.txt* for a text file.) Previous versions of file naming conventions such as in Microsoft FAT (File Allocation Table) for DOS limited the file name to eight characters with a three-character extension delimited by a period (dot) between the file name and extension. Support of long file names makes file management more user friendly and enables creation of large file sets within a single file organization.

For the Unix operating system, file names may be case sensitive. Use of special characters such as an asterisk (*), ampersand (&), percent symbol (%), dollar sign ($), bar (|), caret (^), slashes (/ \), and tilde (~) is discouraged since Unix may interpret special characters as commands. Likewise, use of a hyphen (-) is permitted within the file name but not as the first character of the name. For Windows environments, special characters such as slashes (/ \), colon (:), asterisk (*), question mark (?), quotes ("), less than and greater than (< >), and bar (|) are not permitted. Converting Unix file names to Windows format requires substitution for these special characters with standard characters.

A file extension descriptor such as *.doc* for a Word document is useful for file management by users, but may also be used by the operating system's file management for associating file names with specific applications. A file with a *.ppt* extension, for example, is associated by the Windows file manager with the Microsoft PowerPoint application, while a file with an *.exe* extension is interpreted by file management as an executable application. In some Unix systems, a "magic number" is embedded at the beginning of a file to provide application association.

A file name resides within an overall file system, typically organized within a hierarchical naming structure of directories or folders. Applications may organize their respective files through default subdirectories within the file system to simplify access for the user.

2.2.2 File Ownership

A file's metadata may include access control information on file ownership to manage access. File ownership attributes are a security feature to enforce access rights, particularly in shared environments. Windows 2000, for example, provides a security identifier (SID) that associates specific files with individual users to monitor ownership. Ownership may be restricted to an individual user or extended to a group, but in the latter case additional mechanisms are required to prevent file corruption if multiple copies of the same file are accessed and modified concurrently.

2.2.3 Read/Write Permission Attributes

A file may be designated as read only for individuals or groups, or read and modify/write, as well as no access for sensitive data such as system files. A file that is designated as read only may be shared with others and written back as a duplicate under a different file name for later editing. At the application layer, the permission attributes in a file's metadata may be used to enforce read/write authority and to prevent, for example, a read-only user from changing a file's content. Extending write permissions to an entire group of users creates the possibility that multiple users will attempt to modify a file's contents simultaneously. *File locking* algorithms may be used to ensure that only one edit is allowed or that multiple edits can be accommodated on the basis of time stamping.

2.2.4 Time Stamping

File metadata may include information on when a file was created, last accessed, and last modified. In addition to facilitating file tracking by users, time stamps enable automated processes such as file backup to streamline operations by only processing more recently modified files. Time stamping is also useful for monitoring periods of access so that policy-based mechanisms can determine the age of a data file for archiving purposes.

2.2.5 File Size

File attributes also include the size of a file, expressed as length in bytes. Maximum file size is dependent on the specific file system used, but ranges from 2 gigabytes for earlier versions of Microsoft FAT (FAT16) to a theoretical maximum of 16 exabytes for Windows NTFS. Linux file systems can accommodate file lengths up to approximately 4 terabytes. The file length attribute does not specify where the file's data actually exists on disk media, but simply indicates the file length as of the last modification.

The file system specifies fixed allocation units or file blocks to accommodate a file's contents. File system block sizes may range from 512 bytes to 256k bytes or larger, depending on application requirements. For storage purposes, file system blocks are composed of contiguous ranges of typically smaller (512 byte) disk blocks. Large graphic files would benefit 512k byte file system blocks. A 2MB file would only require 4 blocks. A small file with only 2k of data, however, would waste 510k of space. File system block sizes are therefore established to balance the performance requirements of the applications supported with the most efficient utilization of storage capacity.

2.2.6 File Data Location

If a file's user data were immediately bound to its metadata in a single entity, it would be impossible to efficiently organize and access thousands of files on a single system. Consequently, most implementations of file metadata separate the file monitoring and control information from the file data itself to facilitate specific file search criteria. Having a list of short file metadata records that includes a file size, for example, accelerates searches to identify files over one megabyte in length. Except for small files in Windows NTFS, file metadata includes fields to indicate the location of the file's data on disk, either by listing the disk blocks that contain that data or by giving a pointer to the first block of a file's data. Additional pointers at the end of each relevant data block indicate the next block that was allocated for the file's data, until the last allocated block is reached.

2.3 Systematic Organization of Files

Individual applications rely on their own executable and parameter files as well as the data files on which they operate. A word processing application, for example, may consist of several dozen runtime files and hundreds of associated user documents, templates, and help file. Depending on the number of applications it hosts, an operating system may have thousands of executable and auxiliary files just to implement system operation and management, and hundreds of thousands of application and user data files. The systematic organization of file structures is therefore essential for the efficient operation of the computer system and its applications. Operating systems manage file organization though *file systems*, and file systems, in turn, leverage the metadata of individual files to facilitate the arrangement of files and retrieval of file content.

2.3.1 File System Hierarchy

A file system brings order to the potential chaos of file overpopulation by organizing files into a logical hierarchy. The file system provides a treed structure built on a foundation of a main or *root* directory. The root directory branches into multiple subdirectories that in turn may contain additional subdirectories as well as file entries. As shown in Figure 2.1, applications in Windows environments are generally grouped within a Program Files subdirectory, which contains its own subdirectory entries for individual applications. This nested organization facilitates human navigation through the mass of files on a computer system (although, unfortunately, not all human users fully exploit the capabilities of the file system to logically organize their data files).

2.3.2 Parsing the File System

The treed root and branch structure of file system directories is typically based on an underlying *B tree* (or B+ tree) algorithm that allows each branch to have multiple nodes. The purpose of the B tree method is to streamline searches for individual file entries and reduce the time required to locate a file on disk.

As shown in Figure 2.2, a directory structure based on more than two entries per node accelerates the search process. In this example, allowing only two entries for each branch creates four layers that must be traversed before the file entry is found. Allowing three branch points shortens the search process to three steps. The B tree directory structure does not contain the complete metadata of each file entry, but provides pointers to the location of the file's metadata in a master table.

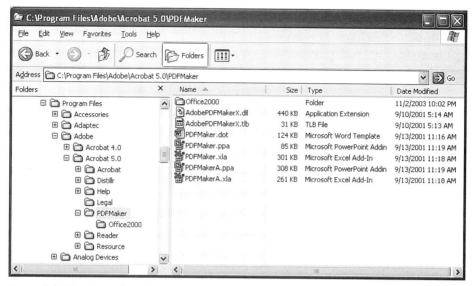

Figure 2.1 The hierarchical placement of files into directories and subdirectories facilitates file organization and retrieval.

2.3.3 Master Tables

Overall file system management requires consolidated information on the file entries, space they occupy, number of total entries allowed, and the storage capacity (free space) the file system has at its disposal. In Unix file systems, this information is recorded on a specific area of disk storage known as the *super block*, which is followed by the inode list of file metadata.

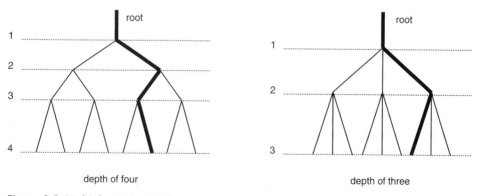

Figure 2.2 Multiple entries per branch point shortens the depth of search.

Inode entries are monitored by file system software and freed for reuse as files or directories are deleted. In Windows NTFS, the *master file table* (MFT) is the repository of file metadata entries as files and directories are created, modified, or deleted.

A file system hierarchy treats both files and directories as file records. A record entry contains the name of the directory or file, but does not specify the complete path to that entry within the system hierarchy. The path, e.g., /usr/src/cmd/date.c, is reconstructed from the tiered directory entries that give the name of the current subdirectory and its parent directory one layer above. Although additional processing is required to generate the full path name, this scheme minimizes the amount of space taken in each file system entry.

2.3.4 File System Integrity

Because the file system has oversight for every change in a file's data or metadata, safeguards are required to ensure the integrity of both the file system itself and the data under its control. A file system is memory-resident code and therefore susceptible to system failures such as power outages or memory faults. If a change to a file has been cached in memory but not updated on physical disk, a system failure would result in corruption of the file's metadata and possibly data as well. Consequently, some file system implementations maintain a second copy of file metadata as a mirror that can be used to restore the file system in the event of failure, maintain separate change logs as an intermediary step before metadata updates, or expedite writing of metadata changes to disk.

When a system failure occurs, the questionable state of the file system is examined by auxiliary utilities that at least identify and hopefully overcome file system corruption. The check disk (chkdsk) utility in Windows and the file system check (fsck) utility in Unix, for example, compare the existing state of the file system master record with its previously saved redundant copy and attempt to restore the integrity of the file system. Attempt is the operative word here, however, since it is always possible that the consistency of some files cannot be recovered.

2.3.5 File System Strategies

File systems are an integral component of operating systems but are not necessarily co-resident with a host platform. The metadata that file system software uses to track changes may reside on locally attached disk, be hosted on a local LAN, or be provided by a storage network. A network-attached storage (NAS) server, for example, supports a shared file system that is accessed through network file system (NFS) or common Internet file system (CIFS) protocols. For NAS, metadata for files and the organization of files into a directory hierarchy are maintained by the NAS server, which is also responsible for file system integrity and more atomic functions such as file locking. Likewise, a SAN-based file system is hosted on SAN-attached storage and made visible to servers over the storage network. The ability to separate file metadata from the file's data content, and separate the governing file system from the compute platform, are preconditions for storage virtualization and create new opportunities for more flexible associations between processors and their data store.

2.4 Chapter Summary

Application Access to Data

- Data is information that has been converted to a machine-readable, digital binary format.

- Control information indicates how data should be processed.

- Applications may embed control information in user data for formatting or presentation.

- Data and its associated control information is organized into discrete units as files or records.

- Files are the common containers for user data, application code, and operating system executables and parameters.

Data as Files

- The control information for file management is known as metadata.

- File metadata includes file attributes and pointers to the location of file data content.

- File metadata may be segregated from a file's data content.

- In Unix systems, file metadata is contained in the inode structure.

- In Windows systems, file metadata is contained in records of file attributes.

■ Metadata on file ownership and permissions is used to control file access.

■ File time stamp metadata facilitates automated processes such as backup and life cycle management.

Systematic Organization of Files

■ A file system is a software layer responsible for organizing and policing the creation, modification, and deletion of files.

■ File systems provide a hierarchical organization of files into directories and subdirectories.

■ The root directory is the foundation of the file system hierarchy.

■ The B tree algorithm facilitates more rapid search and retrieval of files by name.

■ In Unix, the super block contains information on the current state of the file system and its resources.

■ In Windows NTFS, the master file table contains information on all file entries and status.

■ File system integrity is maintained through duplication of master tables, change logs, and immediate writes off file changes.

■ File system recovery is performed through auxiliary utilities such as fsck (Unix) and chkdsk (Windows).

■ File systems may reside on locally attached disks, network-attached storage devices (NAS), or SAN-attached storage.

3

Data on Disk

FILE DATA AND ITS ASSOCIATED metadata control information are managed by the file system. The file system and all the files under its charge, however, are ultimately stored somewhere on physical storage media. In the metamorphosis of data in its file form to data as blocks on disk, additional layers of organization are required to complete the transformation. This chapter examines the intermediate layer of volume management, which provides the bridge between the file system and underlying physical storage, as well as the lower level organization of file data into data blocks.

3.1 Volume Management

File systems reside on volumes of storage. A volume represents the storage capacity of one or more disk drives that has been designated for use by the operating system and its applications. A server, for example, may have one or more storage volumes at its disposal, typically represented by disk identifiers. In Windows, a local volume is referenced as a C: drive; a network-accessible volume may be represented by some other letter, e.g., M: drive. In Unix, the volume identifier is a path to a storage resource such as /dev/dsk1 that is associated with the file system hierarchy by mounting the storage device (i.e., mount /dev/dsk1 /usr).

A volume of storage capacity may map directly to a physical drive, in which case the size of the volume is limited to the size of the drive. This one-to-one mapping would also quickly generate a long list of volume entries as more drives are added to accommodate more capacity requirements. A direct association between a volume and a physical drive also precludes the ability to dynamically add capacity to a volume over time. Consequently, it is desirable to separate the notion of a volume from its underlying physical disk and to represent volumes as logical abstractions of physical storage media. This abstraction also provides transparency for applications in that the physical world can be modified without reconfiguring the application's view of storage.

Logical volume management may be executed as an application that sits between the file system and the device drivers that control system I/O. It may also reside between the computer platform and its target disks, as, for example, a virtualization appliance connected to a SAN. Or, as in the case of RAID controller systems, volume management and the presentation of volumes to a host system may reside in the form of microcode within a disk controller.

In each case, the storage capacity of physical disks is made to appear as something quite different. A large physical drive may be subdivided or partitioned into multiple logical volumes of smaller capacity, as was required by earlier versions of Windows (e.g., FAT16) that could not accommodate multiple gigabytes of storage addressing. Alternately, multiple physical drives may be presented as a single volume, as in the case of RAID systems that write a file's data across multiple disks to improve performance and availability.

Volume management is responsible for creating and maintaining control information or metadata about storage capacity, translating between what the file system sees in the form of logical volumes it has been assigned and the actual physical storage media below. Volumes thus represent an archetypal form of storage virtualization, screening the upper layer applications from the intricacies of the underlying configuration of disk assets.

3.2 Data as Blocks

The unit of currency for the file system that sits on a volume is the file system block. A file system block is a contiguous unit of capacity measured in bytes. The block size is fixed during the creation of the file system and can be configured for as few as 512 bytes up to 512K bytes or more, depending on the requirements of the data being stored. Larger file system block sizes facilitate data access in that more data can be written or read in a single operation. Large file system block sizes, however, may result in unused storage capacity, particularly when small files or records are stored. A volume with an 8K file system block size, for example, would devote 8K of capacity to a file containing only 32 bytes of data. A file with 20K of data would occupy three 8K file system blocks, resulting in 4K of unused storage. Conversely, smaller block sizes are less suited for data access of large files such as graphics or video. A file with 128MB of data would require several hundred thousand 512 byte blocks, but only a few thousand 64K size blocks.

As the discrete unit of allocation within a file system, a fixed size file system block is the smallest container for holding a file's data. Because most files are larger than the designated file system block size, a file's data will span multiple file system blocks within the volume. Each file system block is a contiguous area of physical disk capacity, but the file system blocks containing a single file's data are not necessarily contiguous on disk. A file's data may be dispersed throughout a volume on multiple, randomly situated file system blocks on a single disk or distributed over multiple disks.

Although the file system deals with larger allocation units that can be sized to application requirements, disks have a typical fixed block size of 512 bytes. To properly align file system block size to disk block size, the file system block size is necessarily a multiple of the underlying disk block unit. Each file system block of 16k bytes, for example, would be composed of a consecutive range of 32 disk block numbers, which in turn would correspond to physical sector locations on the disk media.

3.3 The SCSI Protocol and Logical Units

The file system tracks the file's data content via inode or file table block number entries. These blocks, in turn, are initially organized by the volume manager and exist on one or more physical disks. Because the physical disk capacity is segregated from the host system CPU and memory, an external call or input/output (I/O) operation is required to send or retrieve the data blocks. In open systems environments, the protocol that performs the orderly placement or retrieval of data blocks on physical media is the small computer systems interface, or SCSI. The SCSI protocol is responsible for reliable block data transport between host and storage and is implemented in a client/server model between the two.

The SCSI protocol operates below the file system and volume management and above the physical distribution of data blocks on disk, responding to upper layer requests to send or retrieve blocks of data from a peripheral device. A user, for example, may update an online order entry and save the new information. The database application thus initiates a write request to the operating system to store data, and the operating system, in turn, issues a SCSI write for the requisite data blocks to be written. The SCSI protocol does not define how, specifically, the data blocks will be stored once the data arrives. Its task is to oversee the block transfer and ensure its successful completion.

3.3.1 Logical Units

The client/server functions of the SCSI protocol are split between the computer processing platform (initiator), which hosts the SCSI application client, and the storage device (target), which supports the SCSI device server. The SCSI command processing entity within the storage target represents a *logical unit* (LU) and is assigned a logical unit number (LUN) for identification by the host platform.

By convention, SCSI targets are configured via a three-part bus/target/ LUN descriptor, which dates to the original connectivity and cabling scheme of parallel SCSI devices. The bus designator is one of several SCSI interfaces that may be installed on a host system. A traditional parallel SCSI adapter card, for example, may represent a single bus, with that bus supporting multiple daisy-chained disks (targets). Alternately, a Fibre Channel

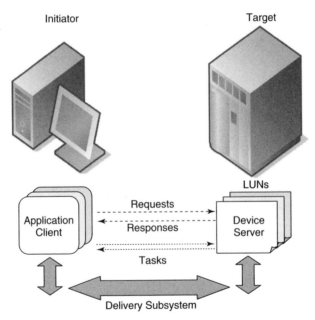

Figure 3.1 SCSI client-server model. The storage target may support multiple logical units and instances of SCSI transactions concurrently.

host bus adapter (HBA) or iSCSI network interface may be viewed by the operating system as a SCSI bus. Multiple installed adapter cards would be seen as multiple bus numbers. The target represents a single storage resource on a bus daisy chain, while the LUN designation identifies the SCSI device server within the target. A single physical disk, for example, may have one logical unit, and consequently one logical unit number. A RAID controller attached to a bus may represent a single bus and target, but have multiple logical units and multiple logical unit numbers (LUNs) assigned.

The bus/target/LUN triad identifier also may be mapped to the addressing requirements of a specific SAN transport. The Fibre Channel Protocol, for example, maps a bus/target/LUN to a device ID/LUN pair, while iSCSI uses iSCSI Target Nodes and LUN designators. Consequently, the representation of the path to physical storage has two components. One is directed at the operating system to establish a familiar addressable entity based on the SCSI triad. The other is directed at the specific storage networking transport, to accommodate the addressing requirements of that topology.

The logical unit represented by a particular LUN is a processing entity within the storage target and is responsible for maintaining the integrity of SCSI read and write operations initiated by a host system. A storage target may support multiple LUNs (up to several thousand in some large disk arrays), enabling multiple servers to share a common storage asset. To accommodate different storage needs, LUNs may be individually sized to the storage capacity requirements of specific operating systems or applications. Storage administrators in large enterprises bear the burden of tedious provisioning of LUNs as new servers and applications are added or resizing of LUNs to meet new capacity requirements of specific servers. Automating LUN management is thus one of the more highly desirable and humane goals of storage virtualization.

Although a logical unit represents an essential part of the client/server SCSI relationship, some liberties can be taken with the number assigned to it. Operating systems, for example, expect to boot from LUN 0. For multiple servers to boot from the same disk array, the array would therefore have to support multiple LUN 0s. This is accomplished by mapping actual LUN numbers on the array to virtual ones, either in the host bus adapter (HBA), the SAN switch, or the target controller. An actual LUN 5 can thus be displayed to one host as a virtual LUN 0, while LUN 6 is presented as a virtual LUN 0 to a different host. In this case, both servers are satisfied with their respective LUNs but mapping adds an additional layer of management oversight for storage administration.

LUN mapping implementations typically include *LUN masking*, or the ability to restrict a server's view of storage to only specifically designated LUNs. This prevents particularly unfortunate occurrences such as, for example, a Windows server seizing and writing a disruptive signature to a LUN originally assigned to an unsuspecting Solaris server. Without some means to hide unauthorized LUNs from the more voracious Windows, the storage data of other operating systems would be a risk. LUN masking also provides a layer of security by enforcing, for example, segregation of data access between different departments that are sharing a large disk array.

A file server or workstation may be assigned multiple LUNs within a storage target and support multiple storage transactions concurrently. The SCSI client-server relationship supports multiple request-response exchanges by generating additional instances of the client-server pair. A large write operation, for example, may be queued with a smaller read request. Because the storage target requires time to receive the incoming blocks of data, coordinate disk head movement over the appropriate disk sectors, and actually write the data to physical disk, it would be inefficient to process the entire write request before attempting to service the read request. *Context switching* enables a host to quickly switch from one job to another to maximize throughput and ensure that all outstanding requests are efficiently processed. Status and diagnostic functions for ongoing SCSI transactions are supervised through task management between the client and server entities. Typically, context switching is performed by the host adapter card, whether it is a parallel SCSI, Fibre Channel HBA, or iSCSI driver.

3.3.2 The SCSI Architectural Model

The overall relationship between SCSI initiators and targets is defined in the SCSI Architectural Model (SAM-2) shown in Figure 3.2. For networked storage, additional NCITS and IETF standards documents further define serial SCSI implementations. Serial SCSI implementations such as Fibre Channel, serial-attached SCSI (SAS), and iSCSI are a component of the SAM-2 definitions for SCSI-3 commands.

The SCSI Architectural Model clearly separates the protocol-specific layer from the underlying transport or interconnect. The client-server requests and responses are exchanged across some form of physical transport, which is governed by the appropriate SCSI-3 service delivery protocol for that transport, such as Fibre Channel or iSCSI for gigabit serial links. The SCSI-3 commands that service I/O requests from the host application are

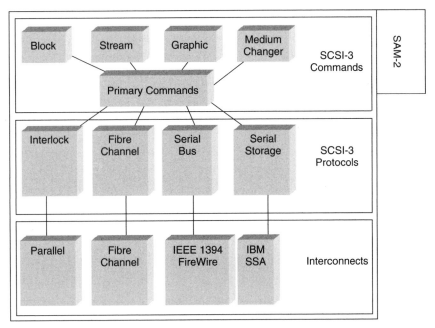

Figure 3.2 SAM-2 SCSI-3 standards functional layers separate underlying interconnects from upper layer protocols and command sets.

thus differentiated from the lower SCSI-3 transport protocols that actually move data via the service delivery subsystem.

This stratification of the architectural model is structured so that the I/O requests from the host system can be serviced without regard to the underlying transport. A single file server could therefore conduct I/O operations against a variety of target types. A server could, for example, have direct-attached SCSI targets as well as serial SCSI targets over a Fibre Channel or Gigabit Ethernet interface.

3.3.3 SCSI Command Descriptor Blocks

The reads and writes of data between SCSI initiators and targets are performed with a series of SCSI commands, delivery requests, delivery actions, and responses. SCSI commands and parameters are specified in the Command Descriptor Block (CDB). The CDB is part of a command frame sent from initiator to target. For improved performance on write operations, the frame may also contain data to be written to the media. Serial SCSI transport protocols such as Fibre Channel and iSCSI simply encapsulate CDBs as their payload. The CDB is encapsulated within the Fibre Channel Protocol Information Units (IU), while in iSCSI it is carried in the iSCSI Protocol Data Unit (PDU).

The first byte of a CDB is an opcode that specifies the type of operation the target is to perform. A SCSI write to disk, for example, triggers the creation of an application client on the initiator (e.g., a host bus adapter in a server), which in turn issues a SCSI command request to the target to prepare its buffers for data reception. The target device server issues a delivery action response when its buffers are ready. The initiator responds by sending blocks. Depending on the lower layer delivery subsystem, the blocks may be transported as bytes in parallel (e.g., low voltage differential SCSI cabling) or segmented into frames for serial transport (e.g., Fibre Channel or iSCSI).

From the standpoint of the application or operating system, the write was conducted as a single operation. In reality, a single write may cause multiple delivery requests and delivery action exchanges before all data is finally sent to the target as shown in Figure 3.3.

In a read operation, the SCSI command block reverses the sequence of data delivery requests and acknowledgments, although it is assumed that since the initiator issued the read command, its buffers are ready to receive the first set of data blocks. The number of blocks sent in a single phase of write or read transactions is negotiated between the initiator and target and is based on the buffering capacity of each. High performance disk arrays, for example, typically provide large buffers to accommodate larger transfers and thus increase productivity.

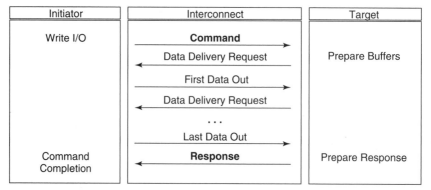

Figure 3.3 A SCSI write operation with multiple data delivery actions to complete a single command/response pair.

3.4 Block Aggregation

The SCSI protocol and supporting client/server relationship is responsible for the orderly transport of data between the host system and its storage target. The data itself is organized as blocks of contiguous streams of bytes of a predetermined length. Depending on the physical configuration of disk drives, the data blocks that compose a SCSI transaction may be written to a single large disk or dispersed across multiple disks in an array. Determining how, specifically, the data blocks should be stored is a factor of cost, performance, and data integrity requirements.

The distribution of data blocks to disk may be under the control of the host system, a virtualization appliance attached to a SAN, or disk controller logic as part of a storage array. Techniques for block placement on disk have been canonized in the form of various RAID (redundant array of independent disks) levels that have been designed to offer different performance and recovery capabilities.

Because disk drives have both mechanical and electronic components that are often in continuous operation, the eventual failure of an entire disk or corruption of disk media sectors is simply a matter of time. Improvements in disk drive technology have increased the mean time to failure, but finding means to compensate for eventual failures is a requirement for data integrity. In addition, access rates for disk drives are far slower than computer memory, resulting in a perpetual performance bottleneck as data moves to and from memory to storage. RAID options attempt to address both reliability and performance issues.

3.4.1 RAID 0

RAID 0 provides no redundancy (which gives it its zeroed status) but does address the issue of disk latency. When a server is connected to a single disk drive, reads or writes of multiple data blocks are limited by the buffering capability and rotation speed of the disk. While the disk is busy processing one or more blocks, the host must wait for acknowledgment before sending or receiving more data. While this delay may be acceptable on an individual PC or workstation, it imposes too much latency for servers that are attempting to accommodate multiple user requests.

As shown in Figure 3.4, throughput can be increased by dispersing data blocks across several disks in an array, a technique called *striping*. In a write operation, for example, the host can send fewer data blocks to multiple

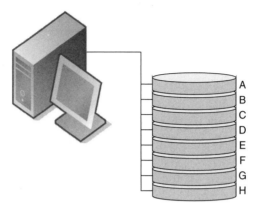

Figure 3.4 Striping data blocks across multiple disks improves performance but provides no means to recover data if a disk fails.

targets consecutively and avoid swamping the processing capacity of any individual disk drive. While one disk is processing blocks it has received, the next disk in line is receiving the subsequent blocks from the server. This simplified RAID 0 boosts performance, but does not provide data security. If a single disk fails, data cannot be reconstructed from the survivors.

Typically, a RAID 0 stripe is driven by a host system to a group of disks that may be directly attached or connected via a SAN transport. A JBOD (just a bunch of disks), for example, has no front end controller or processing intelligence for the array and each disk is recognized and addressed individually by the host system. The host server is therefore responsible for sending blocks to each disk in sequence and monitoring the completion of each write operation.

Because RAID 0 provides no disk redundancy, it is not usually implemented for mission-critical applications. It may, however, be supplemented with mirroring to provide both performance and recoverability of data.

3.4.2 RAID 1

True RAID redundancy is provided by RAID 1 disk mirroring. RAID 1 may be implemented with just two disks, a primary and a secondary. Every write operation to one disk is duplicated to a second disk, resulting in two identical copies of block data. If the primary disk fails, data can be retrieved from the secondary.

Without striping, however, RAID 1 only achieves recoverability at the expense of write operation performance. As with single disk storage, the buffering capability and disk access time of the disks may result in additional latency as the server waits for both disks to complete each block write processing. Read operations can be enhanced via RAID 1, however, by allowing the initiator to access both disks concurrently.

3.4.3 RAID 0+1

RAID 0 and RAID 1 can be combined to optimize both performance and data recovery in the event of failure, as shown in Figure 3.5. This solution doubles the cost of storage, however, since two sets of disks are required.

The RAID striping and mirroring functions may be supported directly by the host system or by a disk controller front-ending the individual disks. In the later case, additional control logic may initiate data recovery to hot spares if a disk fails. If, for example, a disk in the primary fails, the server can switch to the mirror array to resume data access. In the meantime, data can be synchronized and restored to a hot spare in the primary so that the primary can again resume its role.

3.4.4 RAID 5

Other RAID levels introduce data recoverability by either writing parity data to a dedicated drive or writing parity information on each drive in an array. Parity is calculated on the blocks written to disk so data can be reconstructed from parity information if an individual disk fails. RAID 3

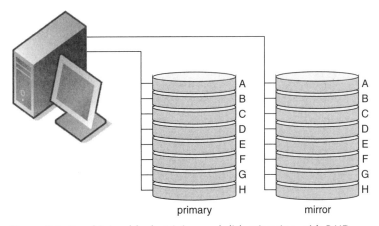

Figure 3.5 Combining block striping and disk mirroring with RAID 0+1 enhances performance and enables data recovery in the event of disk failure.

writes byte-level parity to a dedicated drive. RAID 4 writes block-level parity to a parity drive. Since a dedicated drive contains the information required to reconstruct data, RAID 3 and 4 pose a data integrity problem if one of the data drives and the parity drive fail. RAID Level 5 addresses this problem by striping block-level parity information across each drive. If an individual drive fails, its data can be reconstructed from the parity information contained on the other drives.

The complexity of the parity algorithms for RAID 5 require additional processing power on the storage array and so typically incurs a higher cost for RAID 5 storage arrays. This additional cost may be offset by combining sophisticated RAID 5 logic with more inexpensive disk technology on the back end, e.g., using Serial ATA drives instead of more expensive Fibre Channel drives for storage.

3.4.5 RAID Controllers

RAID logic may reside at any point along the path from the server to physical disks. RAID can be implemented by the operating system via disk administration, be supported by a dedicated host bus adapter slotted in a server, or be driven by controller logic as part of the storage array. If the operating system itself manages data striping or mirroring, the host CPU must devote cycles to these tasks. Software RAID on the host thus imposes processing overhead, but this may be an acceptable tradeoff as CPU clock rates continue to improve. For moderate performance requirements, software RAID offers the advantage of economy and the ability to leverage lower cost JBOD storage.

Positioning RAID logic at the storage array, by contrast, makes control over block distribution independent of any individual server. Any server in a failover cluster can connect to the LUNs supported by a failed server and resume data access for clients. The RAID controller sits between the connection path to servers and the trays of disk drives under its control. The outbound interface may be parallel SCSI cabling, Fibre Channel, or iSCSI over Gigabit Ethernet. The backend connection to the disk drives may likewise vary, from SCSI disks to Fibre Channel arbitrated loop disks or Serial ATA or lower cost disks, as shown by Figure 3.6. For higher performance disk access, Fibre Channel is often used. Vixel Corporation (now part of Emulex), for example, pioneered Fibre Channel loop switching ASICs to facilitate high performance backplanes for Fibre Channel-based disk drives.

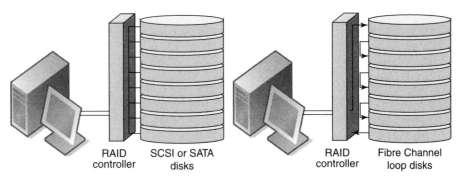

RAID   SCSI or SATA   RAID   Fibre Channel
controller   disks   controller   loop disks

Figure 3.6 A RAID system optimizes performance and reduces overhead for its attached servers and facilitates high availability via server clustering.

Fibre Channel loop has sustained its presence in array architecture since it readily lends itself to high availability via dual loop configurations.

RAID products justify the additional expense compared to JBODs by including high availability and storage management features required for enterprise networking. RAID enclosures may offer redundant, hot-swappable power supplies, redundant fans, and self-diagnostics. Most accommodate online spare drives for auto-reconstruction of data if a disk failure occurs. Large systems can be scaled from hundreds of gigabytes to tens of terabytes of storage, which implies an enterprise-level budget. RAID controllers also typically include large amounts of cache memory to enhance performance. Cache memory buffers data that is being written to physical disks and provides much faster response time for read operations against data that has been recently accessed and cached.

For mission-critical SANs, RAID systems offer a number of advantages. The advanced diagnostics support, management features, reliability, and scalability typical of such high-end systems fill in most of the check boxes for enterprise storage selection criteria. Server processing resources benefit by offloading data redundancy tasks to the RAID controller. Additionally, when the server is freed from the overhead of software RAID, it is also liberated from exclusive ownership of the storage device. Since no single server is responsible for managing the striping of data to multiple disks, any server may own part or all of the RAID controller's data. RAID systems thus enable server clustering and other applications that are predicated on co-ownership of storage resources.

3.5 Getting Data Blocks to Disk

At the file system level, the smallest container for a file's data is the file system block, e.g., 16k bytes. A file of 25k bytes in length would therefore occupy two 16k file system blocks. Because the physical disk may be configured for 512 bytes per disk block, the two file system blocks of 16k each would require 64 disk blocks. Those disk blocks are identified via virtual disk block numbers, which unfortunately have no meaning to the spinning platters and read/write heads flying over them.

At the media level, physical disks simply read and write data in terms of bits laid down on disk sectors, which in turn are defined by head and cylinder position and sector address as shown in Figure 3.7. An additional processing intelligence is required, therefore, to translate between the virtual disk block numbers revealed by the disk controller logic and the lower layer cylinder/head/sector orientation of the physical drives. This function is provided by a lower level microcode that is resident on the physical disk electronics.

When a command to write or read a specific number of bytes beginning at a particular block location is handed off to the disk drive logic, the disk microcode translates the block address into the appropriate cylinder, head, and sector location. The disk seeks to the requisite cylinder by positioning the actuator to place the read/write heads over the cylinder. On multi-platter disks, the appropriate head is then selected. Head selection defines which of the platters will contain the desired data. Because the disk platters are perpetually spinning, the head must track the rotation of its disk to be

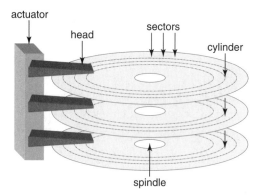

Figure 3.7 Spinning storage media uses cylinder, head, and sector orientation to seek specific locations representing data blocks.

positioned over the appropriate sector. The head maintains its position over the designated cylinder by monitoring servo patterns that have been written in the gaps between disk tracks and identifies the beginning of each track via an index mark. Once the appropriate track has rotated into position under the head, the head is enabled to begin reading or writing data bytes for the specified length.

This fairly straightforward process, of course, becomes an engineering challenge when the disk platters in question are spinning at 10,000 revolutions per minute and the recording density approaches 30,000 data bits per millimeter along the track. As storage expert Richie Lary has remarked, the combination of current disk rotation speeds and low head clearance to platters (13 nanometers) is equivalent to flying a Boeing 747 at 3 million kilometers per hour at a sustained height of one-fourth of a millimeter above, hopefully, very level ground.

With the bytes of user data now successfully secured on storage, we have completed the journey of data movement from application to file system, volume management, LUNs, block aggregation, and physical disk media and processed that data from its file and record format to data blocks on disk. For write operations, this transformation occurs in one direction; for reads, in the opposite direction. At every step, some form of virtualizing has occurred, albeit on a fairly atomic level. Storage virtualization is dependent on these underlying abstractions, but extends the separation of logical and physical to a higher level. How this is accomplished will be discussed in the following chapters.

3.6 Chapter Summary

Volume Management

- A volume represents the storage capacity of one or more disk drives.

- Logical volume management may sit between the file system and the device drivers that control system I/O.

- A large physical drive may be subdivided into multiple logical volumes.

- Volume management is responsible for creating and maintaining metadata about storage capacity.

- Volumes are an archetypal form of storage virtualization.

Data as Blocks

■ The atomic unit of file system management is the file system block.

■ A file system block is composed of a consecutive range of disk block addresses.

■ A file's data may span multiple file system blocks.

■ File system blocks containing a file's data content may be dispersed over multiple physical disks.

The SCSI Protocol and Logical Units

■ The exchange of data blocks between the host system and storage is governed by the SCSI protocol.

■ The SCSI protocol is implemented in a client/server model.

■ The SCSI protocol is responsible for block exchange but does not define how data blocks will be placed on disk.

■ The server portion of the SCSI exchange is executed in the target by a logical unit (LU).

■ Logical units are identified by assigned numbers LUNs.

■ Multiple instances of SCSI client/server sessions may run concurrently between a server and storage.

■ SCSI targets are configured via a bus/target/LUN triad descriptor.

■ Large storage arrays may support several thousand LUNs to service multiple clients.

■ LUN assignment can be manipulated through LUN mapping, which substitutes virtual LUN numbers for actual ones.

■ A server's view of available storage LUNs can be restricted via LUN mapping.

■ Running concurrent SCSI transactions is achieved through context switching.

■ The overall relationship between SCSI initiators and targets is defined by the SCSI Architectural Model (SAM-2).

■ SAM-2 delineates between command, protocol, and interconnect layers.

- SCSI commands, status, and data are contained in the Command Descriptor Block (CDB).

- Fibre Channel and iSCSI encapsulate SCSI CDBs for data delivery.

Block Aggregation

- Data blocks may be written sequentially to a large disk or allocated via striping to multiple disks.

- RAID (redundant array of independent disks) is a means to achieve efficient block distribution to achieve performance, recoverability, or both.

- RAID 0 provides performance by striping data blocks across multiple disks in an array.

- RAID 1 provides data recoverability through disk mirroring between a primary and secondary array.

- RAID 0+1 combined both techniques to offer both performance and data integrity.

- RAID 5 writes block data and parity to multiple drives to achieve recoverability of data in the event of a single disk failure.

- RAID can be driven by the host system via software or by disk controller logic on the array.

- Software RAID imposes a performance penalty on the host CPU.

- Array-based RAID provides independence for data assets and enables high availability server strategies such as clustering.

Getting Data Blocks to Disk

- Disk drives read and write data to media through cylinder, head, and sector geometry.

- Microcode on a disk translates between disk block numbers and cylinder/head/sector locations.

- This translation is an elementary form of virtualization.

- Recording density on magnetic disk media is currently around 30,000 data bits per millimeter of track.

4

The Storage Interconnect

SERVERS ATTACH TO STORAGE through a variety of interconnects, including traditional parallel SCSI and serial connections such as Fibre Channel or serial-attached SCSI (SAS). This chapter examines the various types of storage interconnects and how storage virtualization technology can maximize connectivity to support reliable and transparent storage access.

4.1 The Path to Storage

The basic division between internal compute resources and external peripherals requires an input/output (I/O) mechanism for bridging between the host CPU plus its memory and external storage resources. The bus on a CPU motherboard, for example, supports multiple adapter cards for attachment to physical storage. Device drivers hosted by the operating system perform the appropriate protocol conversions to translate SCSI read and write requests from the operating system into the corresponding commands for a specific storage interconnect across the adapter card. Microsoft's traditional SCSIPort driver and more recently introduced StorPort driver, for instance, provide the operating system software interface to complete the storage connection between internal and external realms.

The storage interconnect has both hardware and software components. On the host side, connectivity is enabled by hardware components such as host bus adapters (HBAs) for conventional SCSI or Fibre Channel or network interface cards (NICs) for iSCSI. Each vendor's adapter card is typically accompanied by a vendor-specific software device driver, written to the unique requirements of the operating system's storage driver. The HBA or NIC, in turn, provides the external interface to storage assets via cabling connectors: parallel interfaces for SCSI, optical or copper interfaces for

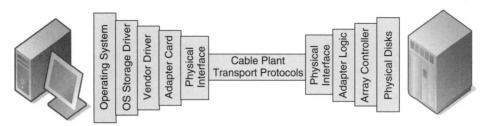

Figure 4.1 The storage interconnect is constructed using both software device driver and hardware components. The cable plant carries the transport protocols responsible for data delivery.

Fibre Channel or Gigabit Ethernet. Along the cable plant, transport protocols execute the delivery of commands, status, and data between the host and its external storage targets as shown in Figure 4.1. The connectivity may be directly to a storage asset or to a storage network supporting multiple storage assets.

Because storage transactions are often mission-critical, storage network design typically incorporates dual pathing between servers and storage. This is accomplished by provisioning dual HBAs or NICs in the server and enabling a multi-path device driver that monitors the status of both links. In the event of failure of one adapter card or link, software selects the still active alternate path.

For true high availability, however, providing dual paths from the server must be supplemented with dual links along the entire path from server to storage. Installing two Fibre Channel HBAs in a server with connections to a single fabric switch, for example, would only provide redundancy at the HBA and server link level. The failure of the switch would bring down both paths. Consequently, dual pathing normally requires redundancy within the SAN: dual HBAs, separate links to redundant Fibre Channel switches, and separate links from the fabric to separate ports on the storage target. Fibre Channel directors mitigate this requirement by typically providing five-nines (99.999%) availability. Dual paths from a server to a director, however, should provide attachment to separate line cards in the director chassis.

4.2 Storage Ports

Storage arrays provide external interfaces for connectivity to servers or storage networks. The outward interface may be parallel SCSI, Fibre Channel, Gigabit Ethernet, serial-attached SCSI, or other interfaces, but is typically

Fibre Channel for higher end arrays and SCSI for mid to low-end arrays. Large storage arrays may support 64 or more ports for external connection. Each vendor has its own best practices recommendations for proper fan-out ratios between a storage port and the servers aggregated to it.

Each storage port has processing logic that is responsible for executing the appropriate transport protocol for the storage connection. Because the transport protocol (e.g., SCSI, Fibre Channel, or iSCSI) is standards-based, there is little opportunity for proprietary value-add at the storage port. At the most, vendor differentiation may be in the number of concurrent devices and sessions that can be supported per port. Fibre Channel storage ports may be at 2 Gbps or 4 Gbps, with raw bandwidth facilitating a larger number of servers per port. Both Fibre Channel and iSCSI technologies are driving toward 10 Gbps port interfaces, which will somewhat level the playing field between the two protocols and enable a much higher fan-out ratio of servers to storage port.

Behind the storage ports, the array controller logic, cache, and auxiliary processors negotiate between the inbound server sessions and backend storage disks. The controller logic implements the appropriate RAID levels and sets that have been established through administration. As discussed in Chapter 3, RAID is an elementary form of storage virtualization and provides an abstraction layer that presents multiple physical disks as a single logical disk. From the RAID sets created via administration, the storage array displays logical disks in the form of logical unit numbers (LUNs) that may be accessed by client servers. LUNs are typically sized to the capacity requirements of individual applications on servers. LUN masking and LUN mapping may also be provided by the array to simplify and secure server SCSI sessions.

The transport protocol running over the outbound interface of the storage port is independent of the protocol supported by the array's backend disk drives. An array may present Fibre Channel for server connectivity, but provision traditional parallel SCSI disk drives for storage. The independence between the storage port and physical disks provides flexibility both in terms of array design and cost. Physical disks may vary in cost from higher performance Fibre Channel loop drives to traditional SCSI drives or more economical drive technology such as ATA (advanced technology attachment, also referred to as IDE or integrated drive electronics) or serial ATA (SATA). The capacity, performance, and reliability characteristics of storage arrays vary widely but are usually reflected fairly accurately by price. The wide range of array offerings, however, enables customers to select class of storage for different applications or different stages of an application's data lifecycle.

The storage array's controller logic may include an auxiliary virtualization engine for array-to-array storage virtualization. This enables multiple storage arrays to communicate across storage ports and present the ensemble of arrays as a single storage pool. As discussed later in Chapter 7, array-based storage virtualization software is typically proprietary, since in addition to the storage pooling function, vendors wish to preserve their value-added array-based storage services.

4.3 Storage Interconnects

The storage interconnect links the host interface to the storage port over some form of physical cabling plant. Storage interconnects may be parallel direct-connect cabling or serial network cabling. Parallel SCSI interconnects are still widely used today, particularly for medium and low-end storage applications. Serial interconnects such as Fibre Channel and iSCSI over Gigabit Ethernet, however, are enabling media for storage networking and offer many advantages over parallel cabling schemes. Although it is possible to implement forms of storage virtualization over conventional SCSI parallel cabling, serial interconnects provide much more flexibility for connecting diverse storage assets for virtualized solutions.

4.3.1 SCSI Interconnects

Parallel SCSI interconnects have been the mainstay of open systems storage for decades. Because the SCSI protocol for block transactions was developed on the basis of a parallel cabling plant, the term SCSI is bound to its original interconnect. In reality, the SCSI protocol is independent of the underlying transport and willingly performs over both parallel and serial infrastructures.

The original SCSI storage interconnect was a parallel cable with 8 data lines and a number of control lines. Transmitting 8 bits of data during each transmit clock provides a relatively high bandwidth, but electrical issues restrict the total distance allowed by most SCSI implementations to 15 to 25 meters. The SCSI parallel bus architecture has evolved over time, with higher bandwidth provided by wider data paths (16 data lines and 32 data lines) and faster clocks rates.

One of the difficulties presented by parallel bus architecture is a phenomenon known as *skew*. If 8 or 16 bits of data are sent simultaneously in

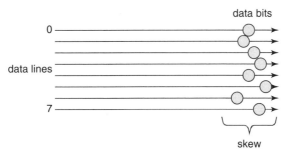

Figure 4.2 Timing skew on parallel bit transmission
is sensitive to the latency of each data line.

parallel, small differences in propagation delay along each data line may occur, and all bits may not arrive at the destination at precisely the same moment. Skew refers to the difference in arrival time for each bit comprising a data word. The skew window is the time difference within which all bits must arrive. As shown in Figure 4.2, the greater the differences in propagation delay, the wider the window must be to ensure that all data bits are captured. The sensitivity to bit propagation has made it difficult to extend parallel SCSI cabling to longer distances. Serial transmission, by contrast, is not subject to skew and this enables serial transports such as Fibre Channel and Gigabit Ethernet to drive the storage interconnect to tens of miles in length.

To accommodate hundreds of gigabytes or terabytes of data, it is necessary to deploy multiple external disk enclosures, which may be connected by parallel SCSI cabling to multiple SCSI host bus adapters installed in the server, as shown in Figure 4.3. Performance for SCSI interconnects has evolved from ~5MBps on the original SCSI-1standard to ~320MBps for SCSI-3 Ultra320. In addition to distance limitations, however, each daisy-chained string of SCSI devices can only support up to 16 SCSI IDs, thus restricting the total storage capacity for direct-attached SCSI interconnects.

For storage virtualization applications, the major drawback of the SCSI storage interconnect is that it binds storage resources to a single server. Although host-based virtualization could create a storage pool from the multiple SCSI arrays on multiple SCSI strings, the virtualized storage would still only be accessible to one server. The failure of that server would make the data on the pool inaccessible to any application clients.

For direct-attached storage configurations, the limitations of parallel SCSI are being addressed by Serial Attached SCSI (SAS). The SAS specification is

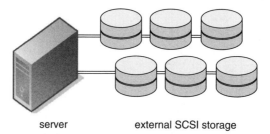

server   external SCSI storage

Figure 4.3 Server with multiple SCSI adapter
cards and SCSI parallel cabling to disks.

being developed by the INCITS/ANSI T10 group as the next generation
direct-attached storage interface. While SAS is not intended as a replacement
for networked storage, it will provide efficiencies in local storage connectivity
and will be immune to the skew and distance limitations of parallel cabling.

4.3.2 Fibre Channel SAN Interconnects

In the early 1990s, the creation of the Fibre Channel architecture introduced a new storage interconnect for attaching storage and servers to a peer
network infrastructure. This technology was so innovative and portended
such dramatic changes in traditional storage relationships that at first no
one could agree what to call it. Thanks to the prompting of Howie Chin
(formerly of the now defunct Gadzoox) and others, within a few years the
acronym SAN became the accepted umbrella marketing term for a diversity
of Fibre Channel networked storage solutions.

Fibre Channel has overturned direct-attached storage interconnects by
enabling serial transport of block SCSI data over a serial network. The term
network applied to Fibre Channel acquires a fairly narrow definition. Fibre
Channel standards do not provide a routing function, as is the common assumption for IP networks. In its fabric flavor, Fibre Channel relies on high
performance switching at the link layer and so is more channel than true
network. A channel, as first implemented in mainframe systems for peripheral access, relies on high-speed links between host and target for delivery of
large blocks of data per transaction. Nonetheless, basic network characteristics such as peer-to-peer communication, scalability to multiple devices on
a single network segment, and data delivery over a serial infrastructure are
found in Fibre Channel standards. Despite the objections of some industry
analysts, usage of the term *network* as applied to Fibre Channel SANs
would probably hold up well in any technology court.

Fibre Channel architecture defines three primary topologies for a storage interconnect: point-to-point, arbitrated loop, and fabric. Point-to-point connections between two Fibre Channel devices are rarely used, and arbitrated loop has been consigned to backend disk drives and backplanes for some storage arrays. Nearly all Fibre Channel configurations today are based on fabric switches and directors at the SAN core, with Fibre Channel interfaces on both servers and storage ports.

Unlike traditional Ethernet networks, Fibre Channel fabrics are predicated on intelligence in the network. In a conventional data communications network, it is assumed that the hosts will be active initiators of transactions. All the network has to do is convenience the communication between end devices and ensure data delivery. In a storage network, by contrast, an end device may be relatively dumb, such as a JBOD enclosure of multiple separately addressable disks. Targets in general are passive, awaiting service requests from initiators such as servers. In order to identify potential targets, a server needs some means of device discovery, and because the target does not advertise itself, the discovery service must be provided by the network. This is the function of the simple name server (SNS) common to all Fibre Channel fabric switches and directors.

In addition, the architects of Fibre Channel wanted to create a self-configuring network that would automatically assign fabric addresses and avoid address duplication. To ensure unique addresses in the fabric, fabric switches themselves assume responsibility for address allocation. When two or more fabric switches are connected, they undergo a fabric building process. The role of principal switch is negotiated between the switches, and once the selection is complete, the principal switch allocates 64k blocks of unique addresses to the secondary switches.

A device that is connected to a switch performs a fabric logon and is automatically assigned a unique 3-byte network address. The device then registers with the fabric's simple name server and informs it of its capabilities. Because targets have registered with the SNS, a newly attached server can query the switch's SNS for the addresses of available targets, and, supposing a target has been authorized for access by that server, the server can begin establishing a storage session with it.

Auxiliary services such as LUN masking, zoning, and state change notification provide more fabric control over communications. Zoning places authorized storage devices and servers into a common communication domain. Devices outside the zone cannot access those within it. This ensures, for example, that a storage array is only accessible by designated servers running Windows, and that Windows servers cannot access Solaris storage. Zoning manipulates the fabric's response to SNS queries by servers, so that only authorized devices are returned.

Registered state change notification (RSCN) is a fabric-based means to alert servers to the entry or disappearance of storage assets on the fabric. Upon receiving a state change notification, for example, a server could query the SNS to see what additional resources are available.

This fabric-based intelligence distinguishes Fibre Channel networks from typical Ethernet networks. In the IP world, automatic addressing may be provided by auxiliary devices such as a DHCP (dynamic host configuration protocol) server. Device discovery may be provided by other external services such a domain name service (DNS) or the service locator protocol (SLP). But these enhanced functions are not typically embedded in silicon on the Ethernet switch or IP router, whereas addressing, discovery, and notification are inherent features of Fibre Channel fabrics.

Because Fibre Channel switches already deliver advanced communication transport services, embedding storage virtualization technology in a fabric switch requires no tremendous leap of faith. Network intelligence is a prerequisite for SANs, and storage virtualization simply represents an extension of that intelligence into the data path. In addition, because the switch provides the data path between servers and storage arrays and tape, it is positioned to intervene in storage transactions and present a logical abstraction of the storage systems. Standards initiatives such as the Fabric Application Interface Standard (FAIS) proposal, for example, are defining common APIs that will enable communication between virtualization engines and the fabric in multi-vendor environments.

Normal Fibre Channel switching imposes minimal processing latency through *cut-through* switching at the port level. Cut-through reads the destination Fibre Channel address in the incoming frame header and begins switching the frame contents to the appropriate egress port. Because the destination ID is within the first 4 bytes of the frame, the switching decision and routing of the remaining ~2k of data begins almost as soon as the frame is received. Although cut-through technology provides the best performance for data movement through the fabric, it has no visibility to the SCSI commands, status, or data encapsulated in the frame payload that is some 24 bytes to 152 bytes (if optional headers are used) beyond the start of frame. To index far enough into the Fibre Channel frame to interpret contents such as LUN addressing, a fabric switch supporting storage virtualization would need to implement a *store-and-forward* switching algorithm or be able to probe frame content on the fly via ASICs. Store and forward buffers the frame before switching it to the appropriate egress port and, while imposing a processing penalty in terms of raw performance, enables the manipulation of Fibre Channel addressing and LUN designations.

Fibre Channel at 2 Gbps provides a theoretical 200 MBps data delivery from source to destination. Actual performance may be somewhat lower, in the ~160 MBps to ~180 MBps range. Moving to 4 Gbps doubles the throughput, although like 10 Gbps Fibre Channel, this improvement is most useful for interswitch links (ISLs) and storage ports. Server performance requirements are typically well below 200 MBps. Higher performance within the fabric and at the storage port provides more efficient plumbing for storage virtualization solutions. Particularly for in-band virtualization, greater bandwidth in the infrastructure compensates for the additional overhead that may be incurred by control and synchronization traffic.

For distance, Fibre Channel at 1 Gbps can run up to 500 meters on standard shortwave optics and cabling (50 micron) and typically up to 10 kilometers with long wave optics and cabling (9 micron). New long wave optical media pushes distance support beyond 10 kilometers to ~50 kilometers or more. Fibre Channel at 2 Gbps is limited to 300 meters on shortwave optics. Achieving greater distances for Fibre Channel traffic requires auxiliary technologies such as dense wave division multiplexing (DWDM), Fibre Channel over SONET (FC-SONET),or IP-based solutions such as Fibre Channel over IP (FCIP) or Internet Fibre Channel Protocol (iFCP). The latter solutions can drive Fibre Channel-originated traffic up to thousands of kilometers. In terms of storage virtualization, support for greater distance facilitates integrating geographically dispersed storage assets for an enterprise-wide virtualization strategy.

A fabric may be built with Fibre Channel switches, Fibre Channel directors, or both. Both switches and directors provide basic fabric services such as logon, SNS, RSCN, and zoning. Switches, however, typically support from 8 to 32 devices. Directors may support 256 or more devices. In addition, although switches may provide redundant fans and dual power supplies, they are not designed for five-nines availability. Directors have full redundancy, including processors and (often) backplanes, and may support advanced diagnostics with phone-home capability for service.

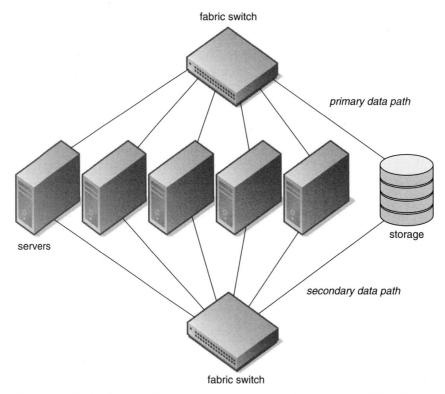

Figure 4.4 Redundant pathing ensures storage access in the event of HBA, link, or switch failure.

As shown in Figure 4.4, a small Fibre Channel SAN is often configured for high availability by deploying redundant connections and switches. If a HBA, server-to-fabric link, storage-to-fabric link, switch port or entire switch fails, each server still has an available path to its storage data. Because the server has two separate paths to storage, however, it also has two images of its assigned LUNs. Software is therefore required on the host to reconcile this duplication and present a single image of storage resources. Path failover in the fabric may be supplemented by server clustering software on the hosts so that the failure of an individual server can trigger the assumption of its tasks by another server in the cluster.

A director-based SAN may provide dual pathing analogous to Figure 4.4, substituting directors in place of fabric switches. Because directors are engineered for five-nines availability, however, it is also possible to provision redundant links to the same director chassis as shown in Figure 4.5,

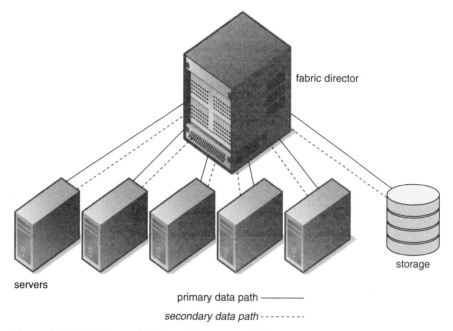

fabric director

storage

servers

primary data path —————

secondary data path - - - - - - - -

Figure 4.5 The high availability architecture of Fibre Channel directors enables alternate means to implement dual pathing between servers and storage.

providing the redundant server and storage connections are made to separate line cards within the director. The failure of an individual component or link would still provide a path to storage.

Fabrics are expanded to provide additional ports by connecting switches or directors with interswitch links. The expansion port (E_Port) connection between switches is analogous to bridging in Ethernet LANs in that the connected switches become a single link layer segment. The more switches in a fabric, the larger the segment. As with bridged LANs, scaling to very large configurations creates the potential for disruption and lengthy network convergence times. This potential has been addressed in Fibre Channel via SAN routing technology, which provides a means to connect multiple SAN fabrics without creating a single extended network segment. With SAN routing, authorized storage conversations are allowed to pass between SANs, but fabric building protocols and state change notification broadcasts are blocked by the SAN router.

The protocols for building extended fabrics via E_Port connections have evolved from proprietary implementations to open systems standards. The switch interoperability issues that plagued early multi-vendor fabrics have now been largely overcome, although the inherent complexity of fabrics and intelligent services requirements make interoperability a constant challenge. Most vendors still provide both vendor-specific proprietary E_Port as well as an open systems mode E_Port. With additional layers of switch-based intelligence in the form of storage virtualization and no clear standardization of virtualization technology itself, interoperability for fabric-based virtualization will be difficult to achieve.

Most fabric switch architectures support multiple interswitch links (ISLs) between switches or directors. Connecting more than one ISL between two switches is known as *trunking* and is analogous to IEEE 802.3ad link aggregation for Ethernet. Trunking may accommodate simple failover from active to secondary ISL or support load balancing to increase bandwidth between switches. As shown in Figure 4.6, directors A and C are connected by multiple ISLs in a trunk. The need for multi-ISL trunking will be alleviated by 10 Gbps Fibre Channel ISLs, although there seems to be no end to the customers' appetite for bandwidth. For high availability, directors A, B, C, and D are configured in a full mesh topology. Each switch has an ISL to the others so the failure of any ISL would still enable switch-to-switch communication through other links.

Figure 4.6 also depicts an ISL connection between director D and fabric switch F. This is a means to extend access to the SAN core to departmental fabric switches that service smaller workgroups of servers and storage. In this tiered approach, switch F is part of the extended fabric, but gains access to centralized resources such as tape libraries through the director mesh. In addition, external directors or switches may also share centralized storage assets via SAN routers, as shown in the diagram for director E and fabric switch G. These external switches maintain their autonomy as separate SANs while the SAN router passes only authorized storage traffic between their attached devices and the SAN core.

Because the Fibre Channel interconnect enables networked associations between multiple storage systems and servers, it is a viable infrastructure for supporting storage virtualization solutions. Regardless of whether those solutions are host-based, network-based, or array-based, the high performance transport and flexibility that Fibre Channel offers for connecting diverse storage assets makes it easier to virtualize storage relationships. Networking, however, is not the sole purview of Fibre Channel, and iSCSI can provide many of its benefits.

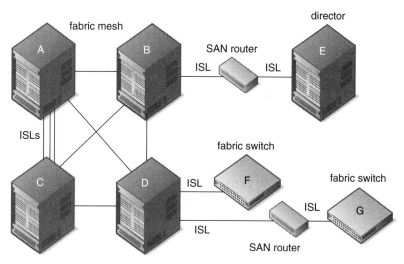

Figure 4.6 Inter-switch links may be provisioned for high availability via meshing and high performance via trunking. SAN routing leverages E_Port connectivity to provide autonomy between connected SAN segments.

4.3.3 iSCSI Interconnects

Like Fibre Channel Protocol (FCP), Internet SCSI (iSCSI) encapsulates SCSI commands, status, and data for block delivery. From the standpoint of the SCSI transaction, FCP and iSCSI perform the same functions for reliable transport from source to destination. Fibre Channel, for example, provides recovery from lost frames by resending an entire sequence of frames. iSCSI recovers lost packets via the TCP (transmission control protocol) layer. FCP is a link layer protocol, with low protocol overhead and optimum performance for data centers. iSCSI uses IP as a layer three routing protocol, performs well over distance and is suitable for departmental applications or second-tier servers. FCP is run over 2 Gbps links, whereas iSCSI transports are typically 1 Gbps or less. FCP requires dedicated interconnects in the form of fabric switches or arbitrated loop. iSCSI can be networked over any common IP infrastructure, although best practices typically recommend using dedicated Ethernet switches and IP links for storage traffic. Aside from these similarities and differences, cost is still a major differentiator between Fibre Channel and iSCSI. iSCSI offers low cost at medium to low performance; Fibre Channel has higher costs but is optimized for high performance.

The iSCSI protocol can operate over standard Fast or Gigabit Ethernet NICs, on accelerator cards with TCP offload engines (TOEs), and on dedicated iSCSI adapters that include both TOE logic and onboard iSCSI protocol processing. For the host connection, cost can range from essentially zero dollars for readily available device drivers for different operating systems, or in the ~$600 range for iSCSI adapters. Flexibility in per-server cost enables iSCSI to bring second-tier, low-cost servers into shared storage.

The iSCSI protocol assumes that both initiators and targets are iSCSI devices. Although iSCSI storage arrays are available for small to medium SAN environments, enterprise-class networked storage is typically Fibre Channel. Fibre Channel currently provides more bandwidth at the storage port for aggregating more initiator sessions per port. In addition, the real estate for interface cards on large arrays is fairly expensive. One of the attractions of iSCSI is its ability to bring lower cost servers into the SAN, so basic economics argue against devoting expensive storage array slots to second-tier servers. Typically, iSCSI servers are accommodated more economically via IP storage switches, which perform iSCSI-to-Fibre Channel protocol conversion. iSCSI sessions through an IP storage switch may be directed to the fabric through E_Port connection, as shown in Figure 4.7, or directly to Fibre Channel storage.

Because iSCSI leverages IP routing, it has no inherent distance limitation. As also depicted in Figure 4.7, support for IP-routed networks makes iSCSI suitable for bringing geographically remote servers into a data center

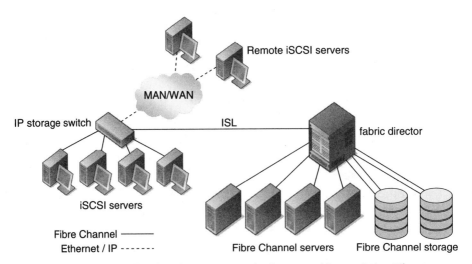

Figure 4.7 Remote and local iSCSI servers may be integrated into existing Fibre Channel SANs via IP storage switches.

SAN. In practice, the available bandwidth on the wide area link and simple speed of light latency will determine the throughput available for iSCSI storage transactions. Upper-layer applications that are sensitive to latency may not perform well over wide area links, but asynchronous applications such as tape backup are relatively immune to latency. In general, transmission latency due to speed of light propagation delay incurs about one millisecond of delay per hundred miles, times two for total round trip latency.

The device discovery, address assignment, and state change services of Fibre Channel fabrics are absent in pristine iSCSI configurations. Gigabit Ethernet switches and IP routers do not provide storage-aware logon services, device registration, query response, or proactive notification for newly introduced iSCSI targets. Consequently, auxiliary protocols are required to convenience initiator-target relationships in iSCSI SANs. The Internet Storage Name Server (iSNS), for example, combines features from Fibre Channel SNS with IP-based DNS (domain name server) services. Upon entering an IP network, servers and storage devices register their presence with an iSNS server at a well-known IP address. The iSNS server may be a network-attached device or an embedded intelligence within an IP storage switch. The iSNS server places newly registered devices into predefined discovery domains, authenticates their identity, and assigns designated iSCSI servers to their authorized storage assets within the IP network. The iSNS server may also be a repository for public key/private key authentication and encryption so that iSCSI sessions may be secured within the network. iSNS client and server software is being implemented in servers by Microsoft and other vendors and scales well for large enterprise IP SANs. Alternately, the service location protocol (SLP) may be used for smaller environments.

As shown in Figure 4.8, one or more iSNS servers may be connected to the IP network to provide device discovery and authentication. Once iSCSI initiators and iSCSI storage targets establish their sessions, however, the iSNS server has no direct involvement in the storage transactions. In Fibre Channel fabrics, by contrast, the fabric switch that provides discovery and other services remains directly in the data path between servers and storage. Because iSCSI separates the services' functionality from storage transactions, it is more dependent on an appliance strategy for additional services such as storage virtualization. Additional network-based intelligence appears in the form of auxiliary boxes connected to the network instead of embedded intelligence in the network's switching apparatus. With further

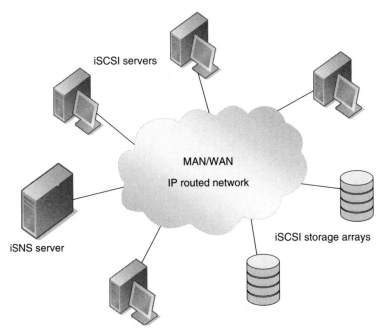

Figure 4.8 In a pure iSCSI environment, initiators discover targets through the iSNS server. Authentication and data encryption secure the storage transactions across the IP-routed network.

convergence of data types within IP transports, however, storage-specific services will begin to appear in mainstream Ethernet switches and IP routers.

Some vendors have already begun to merge iSCSI and storage virtualization services in iSCSI gateway products. Stonefly Networks, for example, introduced an iSCSI gateway that supports both Fibre Channel and legacy SCSI storage devices. A small or medium business could, for example, redeploy their legacy SCSI arrays on the iSCSI gateway and at minimal cost gain the benefits of shared storage. The Stonefly product supports elementary storage pooling so that the recycled SCSI assets can be managed as a single storage resource. In addition, companies like Compellent have introduced modular storage controllers that provide flexibility in iSCSI or Fibre Channel host attachment to virtualized Fibre Channel or low cost storage disks. Such innovations typically come from startup companies and venture capital, but quickly find their way into mainstream storage vendor offerings.

4.4 The Importance of Plumbing

The storage ports, interconnects, transport protocols, and host adapters provide the underlying plumbing on which upper layer storage applications and services such as storage virtualization run. As with other plumbing, the user appreciates its existence but really doesn't want to think about it often. Performance and reliability are therefore essential for keeping the focus on application instead of infrastructure.

Storage interconnects offer a wide range of performance characteristics, ranging from gigabit and sub-gigabit speeds for iSCSI and multi-gigabit speeds for Fibre Channel. High speed at the transport layer accelerates block data delivery and helps compensate for any processing latency introduced by storage virtualization.

The reliability of a transport, however, is far more important for implementing a transparent and robust abstraction layer for storage. Both Fibre Channel and Gigabit Ethernet are proven technologies and, thanks to standardization and interoperability testing, provide a reliable means to move high volume storage data. Reliability is further enhanced by high availability solutions such as alternate pathing, redundant fabrics, SAN routing, and failover between storage ports. Collectively, these mechanisms help maintain the transparency required by storage virtualization by automatically resolving transient disruptions in the storage network. Hiding the complexity of the storage interconnect is a prerequisite for hiding the complexity of the attached storage arrays and tape systems. The user, turning on the tap for a large draft of block data, should not have to listen to the clanging of the pipes in the background.

4.5 Chapter Summary

The Path to Storage

- The storage interconnect provides the data path between servers and storage.

- The storage interconnect is composed of both hardware and software components.

- Operating systems provide storage drivers for I/O to storage assets.

- Storage connectivity for hosts is provided by host bus adapters (HBAs) or network interface cards (NICs).

- For high availability, redundant HBAs or NICs may be provisioned for storage access.

- The cable plant between server and storage may be parallel SCSI, serial optical or serial copper cabling.

- Transport protocols such as Fibre Channel Protocol and iSCSI are implemented end to end for reliable data transport.

Storage Ports

- External interfaces on storage arrays are typically Fibre Channel for high performance or iSCSI for moderate performance requirements.

- The storage port is responsible for executing the appropriate transport protocol for external communication.

- The array controller is responsible for managing backend storage disks, configuration of RAID levels, creation of LUNs, and maintaining storage sessions with initiators.

- The protocols run at the storage port and on the backend disk drives are independent.

- The array controller may support auxiliary processing for array-based storage virtualization.

Storage Interconnects

- SCSI is both a block protocol and parallel cable scheme.

- Skew is the variation in propagation along individual bit lines in a parallel connection.

- Skew limits parallel SCSI connections to approximately 25 meters.

- Parallel SCSI interconnects support from ~5MBps to ~320MBps.

- A parallel SCSI cable plant can support up to 16 SCSI IDs per daisy chain.

- Parallel SCSI imposes exclusive ownership of storage by a single server.

- Serial SCSI (SAS) overcomes the limitations of conventional parallel SCSI.

- Fibre Channel enables peer-to-peer networking of servers and storage devices.

- A Fibre Channel network is a flat, link layer topology.

- Fibre Channel architecture supports point-to-point, arbitrated loop, and fabric interconnects.

- Fibre Channel implements intelligent transport services in the fabric.

- Device discovery in Fibre Channel is provided by the simple name server (SNS).

- Fibre Channel fabrics are self-configuring via fabric building protocols.

- Registered state change notification (RSCN) is a means to alert servers when storage resources enter or leave the fabric.

- The Fabric Application Interface Standard (FAIS) proposal defines APIs for integrating fabrics with storage virtualization engines.

- Cut-through switching begins forwarding frames as soon as the destination address is read.

- Store and forward switching buffers the entire frame before forwarding.

- Standard shortwave optics limit Fibre Channel interconnects to ~300 m.

- Long wave optics can drive Fibre Channel to ~50 km or more.

- Fibre Channel switches are typically 8 to 32 ports.

- Fibre Channel directors may support 256 or more ports and provide high availability features.

- Redundant fabrics provide alternate data paths from servers to storage.

- Fabric are extended via interswitch links (ISL) and E_Port protocols.

- SAN routing facilitates segmentation of storage networks into autonomous SANs.

- Trunking provides multiple ISLs between two switches and may support load balancing.

- Fibre Channel's performance and network infrastructure provides a viable interconnect for storage virtualization.

- iSCSI encapsulates SCSI commands, status and data in TCP/IP.

- iSCSI device drivers can operate over standard Fast or Gigabit Ethernet NICs.

- A TCP offload engine (TOE) performs packet processing on the interface card.

- iSCSI servers can be integrated into Fibre Channel SANs through IP storage routers.

- Device discovery for iSCSI SANs is provided by the Internet Storage Name Service (iSNS).

- iSCSI cost and performance make it suitable for moderate application requirements.

- Some products combine iSCSI with basic storage virtualization pooling services.

The Importance of Plumbing

- Alternate pathing, redundant fabrics, and failover mechanisms provide stability within the storage interconnect.

- Performance and reliability in the storage interconnect are essential prerequisites for storage virtualization.

5 Abstracting Physical Storage

CREATING A SIMPLIFIED, logical view of complex storage assets is predicated on the separation of control information about block data placement and the block data itself. This chapter examines the abstraction layer that enables dispersed physical storage systems to be treated as a common storage pool by manipulating control points for data placement.

5.1 Physical to Virtual

Individual storage systems have internal abstraction functions that mask the physical geometry of backend physical disks and present a simplified representation of storage capacity to external hosts. The host system, for example, may initiate a SCSI I/O to write 10MB of data beginning at a specific storage block address. From the standpoint of the host system, the I/O is performed to a single disk, managed by a single LUN on the target array. From the standpoint of the storage controller, the storage address may in reality be located within a set of disks within a RAID definition. Data blocks that are written to what appears as a single disk entity are instead written to a virtual disk composed of multiple physical disks. What appears as a single SCSI I/O launches a complex series of multiple block data writes in a striping algorithm that may be further tasked with parity generation and verification. At the disk surface, block addressing is translated by the drive logic into the appropriate cylinder, head, and sector coordinates.

The elementary virtualization provided by RAID striping and mirroring relies on one level of abstraction between physical disks and the representation of a virtual disk asset. The agent of that abstraction is the RAID controller logic, which simply presents LUNs composed of a specified number of blocks to the host system. At the system level of storage virtualization, LUNs now become the raw material for manipulation to present entire disk arrays as virtualized resources. A virtualization entity sitting between the storage arrays and the hosts, for example, sees the actual LUNs being advertised by the arrays. In the case of RAID controllers, these storage LUNs are already the product of one phase of virtualization. The virtualization entity can, however, further virtualize the presentation of those storage LUNs by creating virtual LUNs (VLUNs) from the pool at its disposal. A virtual LUN of 20,000 blocks may draw from two separate storage LUNs of 10,000 blocks each. A virtual LUN implemented for mirroring may use two storage LUNs of equal size residing on separate storage arrays.

For JBODs, the virtualization entity may communicate with the individual disk drives within a chassis and thus assume the role of a disk controller. Separate disks can be treated as separate LUNs or grouped into a single or multiple LUNs. A virtualization engine could also stripe data across multiple JBOD disks, acting as a RAID controller. Because JBODs on their own do not have a frontend controller, the creation of virtual disks from real ones must be performed at the host or within the storage network via a virtualization appliance or intelligent switch.

From the host perspective, storage I/O is conducted through device addressing and LUN designators. For Fibre Channel SANs, for example, the conventional SCSI bus/target/LUN triad may be translated by the host bus adapter to a Fibre Channel address and LUN pair. When accessing storage resources directly, the device ID and LUN designation map to the actual ID and LUN assigned for the target. With the addition of a virtualization entity, the device ID may be the virtualization engine on the network and the LUN a fabrication of the virtualizer. The virtualization engine must therefore maintain tables correlating virtual LUNs to real ones on the actual device IDs that it proxies.

5.1.1 Logical Block Address Mapping

The abstraction layer between the host view of storage and the storage itself functions primarily through address-mapping algorithms. A specific storage target, for example, may present a LUN 5 with a storage capacity of 100 gigabytes of data. At 512 bytes per block, there would be 200,000,000 blocks within the LUN's logical block address (LBA) space, ranging from LBA 0 to LBA 199,999,999. In normal usage, a server with access to this LUN would be free to write its data to any of the data blocks. A virtualization engine sitting between the server and the storage target, however, can manipulate both the LUN designation as well as the amount of storage capacity made available to the server. If, for example, only 50 gigabytes of capacity are virtualized to the server, the virtualization intelligence could assign LBA 0 through LBA 99,999,999, or LBA 100,000,000 through 199,999,999 for the server's use, and, depending on whether this LUN is to be a boot resource, assign a virtual LUN designator of LUN 0 or some other identifier. The start and end LBA assignment could, in fact, be anywhere within the target's address space, as long as the total contiguous area equaled 50 gigabytes. The 50 gigabytes could be assigned from LBA 100 to LBA 100,000,099, if for instance a small area of storage was already occupied.

The newly virtualized LUN would present 50 gigabytes of contiguous storage area beginning at a virtualized LBA 0, even if the actual target starting point was LBA 100,000,000 on the underlying storage LUN. If, over time, the server required additional storage capacity, the increase can be accommodated by extending the block space assignment on the underlying target (if available) or by assigning additional blocks from LUNs on a different storage target. In the latter case, the additional blocks would be made to appear as a simple extension (concatenation) of the original virtualized LUN and logical block range. Since the 50 gigabytes on the virtualized storage runs from LBA 0 through LBA 99,999,999, the extended capacity would appear to start at LBA 100,000,000 and run through the requisite number of blocks to satisfy the new capacity requirements.

In Figure 5.1, a virtual volume (VOL2) of 200 gigabytes capacity has been created from LUNs on three different storage units. The first 60 gigabytes is drawn from a Fibre Channel-attached JBOD. The next 40 gigabytes is taken from another JBOD, while the remaining 100 gigabytes are assigned from a RAID system. The virtualized storage runs from LBA 0 through LBA 399,999,999, for 400,000,000 512 byte data blocks. In reality, the actual data blocks taken from each storage system have very different start and end logical block address ranges.

As shown in Figure 5.2, the JBOD at FCID 000400 is contributing blocks from its LBA 0 through LBA 119,999,999, for 120,000,000 data blocks equaling 60 gigabytes of capacity. In this case, the LBA 0 of the virtualized storage corresponds directly to the LBA 0 of the real storage target. The JBOD at FC ID 001100 is supporting the next 40 gigabytes on the virtualized volume, corresponding to the virtual LBA 120,000,000 through virtual LBA 199,999,999. At the JBOD, however, there is a slight offset of 600 blocks before it begins donating to the virtualized capacity. Its starting LBA is LBA 600, running through LBA 80,000,599. Finally, the RAID

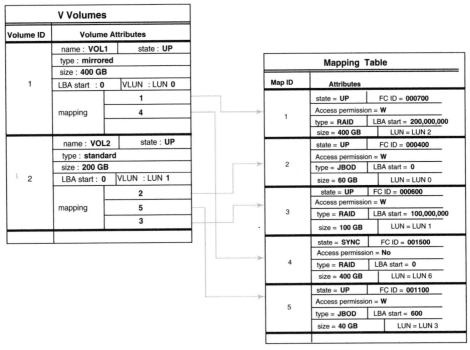

Figure 5.1 What appears as contiguous data blocks on a virtualized storage volume may be composed of dispersed sets of blocks on multiple storage arrays.

system supplies the remaining 100 gigabytes for virtual LBA 200,000,000 through virtual LBA 399,999,999. In this case, the first 50 gigabytes of the RAID has already been assigned elsewhere, so its real starting LBA is 100,000,000 and ending LBA is 299,999,999.

Regardless of where the virtualization intelligence resides, it must maintain the mapping between the virtualized storage entity and the real storage resources composing it. An I/O to write 3 megabytes of data beginning at virtual LBA 134,866,529 must result in a real write operation to FCID 001100 LUN 3 beginning at its LBA 14,867,129. Although the numbers are large, the process is basic math using the appropriate offsets between virtualized locations and real ones.

5.1.2 Virtualized Mirroring

Figure 5.1 also depicts a virtualized volume in a mirrored configuration. As in the previous example, both primary storage and secondary mirror could have been built with multiple storage assets. In this example, though, the

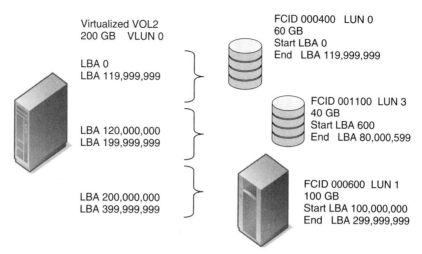

Figure 5.2 Virtualizing storage systems requires mapping algorithms to correlate real sets of data blocks to virtualized sets.

primary is a RAID-based LUN of 400 gigabytes capacity, while the secondary mirror is a JBOD. Because the configuration is mirrored, both the virtualized assets must have equivalent capacity, at least in terms of the storage allocated for the virtual volume. The fact that the primary virtualized storage is RAID-based and the secondary JBOD-based will result in favorable economies in terms of cost, but typically lower performance for the upper layer application. Each write operation must be completed on the JBOD before another I/O can be processed.

Figure 5.3 details a write operation from an initiator to a virtualized storage target over Fibre Channel. The FCP command write is processed by the virtualization engine and sent to both the primary and secondary real targets. This implies that the virtualization entity is target to the initiator and initiator to its downstream underlying storage devices. Data and acknowledgments are passed between the virtualization engine and the physical storage arrays, until all data has been sent, and each real storage unit responds with command completion. Due to the mismatch between the primary storage RAID and the secondary storage JBOD, however, the final acknowledgment of write complete is not issued by the virtualization engine to the initiator until the slower of the two storage devices (in this example, the JBOD) confirms the end of task.

As far as the initiator is concerned, it has only written data to a single storage asset, represented by the virtualization engine. In reality, its data has

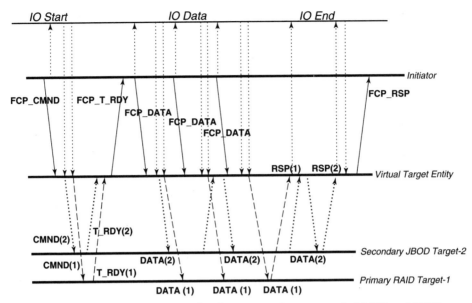

Figure 5.3 Data mirroring to a virtualized storage unit composed of RAID and JBOD may result in lower performance but also lower cost.

been safeguarded via mirroring to two separate storage arrays. The abstraction layer inserted between real initiators and virtual storage thus enables higher levels of data integrity and management without imposing complexity upon host systems. This also transfers ownership of storage data from the server to the virtualization intelligence, since it is the virtualizer that now manages data handling. Depending on higher level policies, the virtualization entity could select the class of storage and quality of service delivery for specific server applications.

5.2 Storage Metadata Integrity

For simplicity in these examples, we have conveniently avoided the issue of where the virtualization intelligence resides, as well as additional responsibilities that the virtualizer may assume. Mapping algorithms to convert virtual block addresses into real ones are common to all virtualization techniques, including host, network, and storage solutions. The mapping information or storage metadata, however, is the sole key to unlock the relationship between virtual storage and real storage. If the storage metadata is lost, access to the real data is also lost. It is therefore necessary to maintain a consistent state of the current storage metadata and additional copies of the current transaction control information (in the previous example, a record of which storage device acknowledgments had been received) either in a standby mode for failover or in a distributed mode for load sharing.

Maintaining storage metadata integrity is complicated by the fact that the virtualization entity may not have full control over all SCSI I/Os. An upper layer application may cache multiple I/O requests before handing them off to the operating system. The operating system, in turn, may have its own I/O cache with queued requests that have not been passed to the host bus adapter. For operations such as snapshots, the virtualization intelligence must ensure that all pending I/Os have been processed before an accurate state of storage transactions can be captured. The mapping component of storage metadata alone can only decipher block placement of data. Additional intelligence and control information is required to ensure consistency of data between the application and its virtualized storage assets.

In addition, other layers of virtualization may be required for specific applications. In the previous discussion of virtualized mirroring, for example, the secondary JBOD mirror could be configured as a striped set. In that case, additional algorithms would be required to associate the logical block address ranges represented by the JBOD with individual block ranges on each JBOD drive.

The virtualizing engine used to associate virtual block address ranges to the blocks actually resident on disparate storage arrays must also be able to handle exceptions on the back end. For RAID systems, some error conditions such as a drive failure may be recovered by the RAID controller itself. For less robust storage targets, however, the responsibility for monitoring and recovering from exceptions falls on the virtualization engine. Compared to the fairly straightforward task of mapping between virtual and real storage systems, implementing fault tolerance in virtualization products is a significant challenge.

5.3 Chapter Summary

Physical to Virtual

- The cylinder, head and sector geometry of individual disks is virtualized into logical block addresses (LBAs).

- A RAID controller further virtualizes individual disks into LUNs with separate LBA ranges.

- Storage system virtualization manipulates LUNs and their LBA ranges to create virtual LUNs (VLUNs).

- For storage networks, the physical storage system is identified by a network address / LUN pair.

- A virtualization engine may assign any range of logical blocks from multiple storage assets to fabricate a contiguous block address range.

- Combining RAID and JBOD assets to create a virtualized mirror must accommodate performance differences.

Storage Metadata Integrity

- Storage metadata must accurately reflect current block address mappings and transaction states.

- Storage metadata integrity requires redundancy for failover or load balancing.

- Virtualization intelligence may need to interface with upper layer applications to ensure data consistency.

- Exception handling is an essential requirement for virtualizing physical storage assets .

6

Virtualization at the Host

VIRTUALIZING EXTERNAL STORAGE ARRAYS can be implemented as a software solution running on host systems. This chapter examines the advantages and disadvantages of host-based virtualization techniques, including logical volume management and pooling of storage assets.

6.1 Logical Volume Management

Servers and workstations typically support some form of storage virtualization through logical volume management. A logical volume manager (LVM) is a software layer that sits between the file system and the operating system's disk driver software, as shown in Figure 6.1. The logical volume manager's tasks may be fairly simple, such as partitioning a large disk asset into smaller and more manageable virtual disks, or fairly complex, such as creating a stripe set of software RAID from multiple physical disks. Volume management utilities may be supplied as part of the operating system, or installed as third-party software (e.g., Veritas).

As with any software utility, the host CPU must do the real work. The additional CPU cycles required for storage virtualization have less impact on today's multi-gigahertz processors than previous generations of CPUs, but more complex algorithms such as software RAID nonetheless impose some processing overhead. Use of host-resident virtualization must therefore be balanced against the processing requirements of the upper layer applications so that overall performance expectations can be met. In addition, because database software and other applications may be licensed on a per-processor basis, the additional cycles consumed by storage virtualization may be an expensive tradeoff.

Logical volume managers are dependent on the efficiency of the operating system and server platform on which they reside and lack specialized

hardware assistance to optimize performance. For modest application requirements, logical volume management performance may be acceptable.
For higher performance requirements, logical volume management may be
complemented by hardware-based virtualization. Software RAID, for example, is rarely used in transaction-intensive applications and high performance is better served by the LVM's management of external hardware
RAID systems.

A primary advantage of server-based volume management is its independence from the unique architectures of external storage targets. The
RAID systems, JBODs, or individual disks under LVM control may have diverse performance characteristics, storage capacities, and availability features. All, however, simply present LUNs to the LVM, which in turn
manipulates LUN representation from these assets to create virtualized storage to the file system or database manager. The heterogeneity implicit in a
storage utility is thus satisfied, although on a per-server basis.

Independence from the unique attributes of storage targets, however,
does not imply indifference to those attributes. In the hierarchy of storage,
all LUNs are not created equal, and a LUN that sits on a RAID 5 array has
superior data integrity characteristics than a LUN presented by a RAID 0

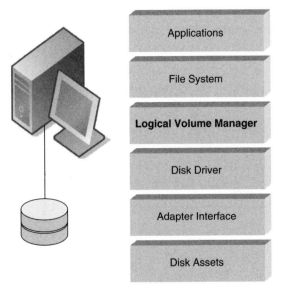

Figure 6.1 The logical volume manager sits
between the upper layer file system and the
underlying operating system disk driver software.

array. Although the logical volume manager can treat any LUN as a vanilla resource for storage pooling, the storage administrator must ensure that the appropriate classes of storage under LVM control are paired with individual application requirements. Although it is enticing to think that low-cost JBODs can be used to mirror more expensive RAID systems, the LVM alone cannot compensate for the lower performance and lower reliability typical of some JBODs.

Logical volume management software usually offers the ability to dynamically size virtualized storage to optimize capacity utilization. Providing the operating system and file system can accommodate expansion or contraction of assigned capacity, an LVM can resize a virtualized LUN and make more or less storage available. Currently, dynamic capacity allocation requires administrative intervention, but at some point additional intelligence between the virtualizing entity and upper layer applications will enable automated resizing of storage assets to align with changing storage requirements.

Logical volume management's ability to virtualize diverse storage targets can also be leveraged for data lifecycle management. Data from one virtualized resource can be migrated to another without disturbing the upper layer application. As data ages and is less frequently accessed, it can be migrated to less expensive storage. Alternately, as an application proves significant value to business operations, its data can be migrated to higher performance and more highly available storage.

Support for dual pathing is another significant benefit of host-based volume management. As shown in Figure 6.2, a LUN represented by SAN-attached storage may be deployed in a redundant configuration with two physical paths between the server and the storage array. At the storage target, two separate SAN ports are associated with the same storage LUN. Those ports are, in turn attached to separate SAN switches. At the server, separate SAN connections are run from different host bus adapters (or iSCSI NICs) to each switch. In this configuration, the failure of a single host bus adapter, link, switch, or storage port would still provide an alternate path to the same storage LUN.

The potential problem of dual pathing, however, is that two separate images of the same storage asset are presented to the server on separate SAN addresses. Without intervention by the logical volume manager, the server would assume that each image represented a unique LUN and SAN address pair. A multi-pathing driver below the LVM layer reconciles this

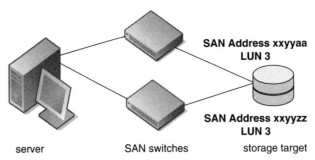

Figure 6.2 Multiple paths between the server and storage
target require reconciliation between the two images of
the same LUN presented to the host.

discrepancy by mapping the two paths to a single LUN. If, for example, a
primary path failed, the second path would be enabled with no disruption
to the file system or upper layer applications.

Dual pathing is mandatory for high availability applications. Despite
the higher cost of provisioning dual HBAs, redundant switches, and additional storage ports, there is no other means to guard against outages
caused by the failure of individual SAN components. Consequently, network diagrams of typical data center SANs are a complex maze of overlap-
ping lines and boxes representing the redundant connectivity between
hundreds of servers and their storage assets. The complexity is compounded
when logical volume management is used to virtualize multiple storage assets, each of which provides dual pathing to individual servers. The LVM
must track both the spectrum of blocks from each physical asset that is used
to generate virtual LUNs as well as the state of redundant pathing to each
physical array.

Because logical volume management is host-based, it must be managed
on each host system individually. For smaller server farms, this may not be a
significant issue, but manual administration of hundreds or thousands of
servers in a large data center can require an army of administrators and
considerable cost. Streamlining storage management through the automation and enhanced policy mechanisms of a storage utility is not feasible
without centralization of virtualization intelligence, and per-server administration precludes centralization. As a result, even traditional vendors of
server-based logical volume management software are pursuing alternatives
such as appliance or fabric-based virtualization.

Another limitation of server-based LVMs is the exclusive ownership of storage assets under LVM control. An LVM that is configured for software RAID of multiple physical disks, for example, is the sole owner of the virtualized resource. If another server attempted to access those disks, it may have no way of knowing how the stripe set is configured and thus no means to read or write data to it. The original owner thus becomes a single point of failure, and data access is lost if the server crashes or is offline. Likewise, although a large storage asset such as a hardware RAID system may be shared by multiple servers running LVMs, each LVM may operate in isolation from the others. Such segregation makes it difficult to coordinate higher levels of storage sharing required for applications such as server clustering. Clustered volume management software is required for coordination between each server's view of external storage to enable clustering and more granular storage sharing.

6.2 Storage Metadata Servers

Traditional logical volume managers evolved on the basis of direct-attached storage and quickly adapted to the new requirements imposed by storage networking. Although traditional LVMs maintain the server-centric view of direct-attached storage, the storage-centric world of SANs is forcing volume management beyond its original confines. Sharing virtualized mapping of physical storage systems between multiple servers not only facilitates asset sharing and server clustering, it also enables distributed file-level sharing via SAN file systems.

A SAN file system presents a common view of virtualized volumes and the upper layer file system sitting on them to multiple SAN-attached servers. As in conventional file systems, each server assumes that it has exclusive control over the supporting volumes. In reality, control is distributed across multiple servers or accessed in common through a storage metadata server. Block allocation is no longer under the ownership of an individual server, but managed in concert for multiple servers.

Theoretically, virtual volume information could be dynamically shared between multiple servers in a cluster, although this would generate significant chatter between servers to maintain a coherent view of virtualized resources. Alternately, as shown in Figure 6.3, the coordination of block mapping metadata may be assigned to a single metadata server. Although this is similar in

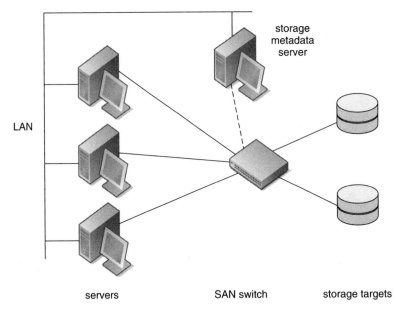

storage
metadata
server

LAN

servers   SAN switch   storage targets

Figure 6.3 The storage metadata server maintains block mapping
information for the virtualized volumes supporting the SAN file system.

approach to out-of-band virtualization appliances, in this case the metadata
server is simply a dedicated server running virtualization software on top of a
common operating system such as Windows 2000; it lacks appliance-like
hardware acceleration and optimization for virtualization.

In Figure 6.3, each server runs a software shim or filter that redirects
I/O requests to the storage metadata server over the local area network. The
storage metadata server responds with the actual SAN address, LUN, and
logical block address data required for the data read or write. The request-
ing server then performs the I/O across the SAN to the appropriate storage
systems using the modified addressing information provided. Although the
storage metadata server is a potential bottleneck for multiple server requests, it offers the advantage of centralized management of the virtualized
assets. Aside from calculating physical block addresses from virtual ones,
the amount of control data that is passed between the servers and the storage metadata server is minimal.

The underlying storage virtualization supplied by the metadata server to
the production servers is meant to support the distributed SAN file system
for common file access. For discrete file sharing, this mechanism also requires a file locking control to avoid data corruption. The difficulty of coor-

dinating file access between multiple servers is compounded by the various means that heterogeneous operating systems use to track file access permissions, file attributes, and time stamps. It is more common to see distributed SAN file systems written for a specific operating system (e.g., Windows) than cross-platform environments.

6.3 Server-Based Storage APIs

Although logical volume management enables servers to virtualize external storage assets, it lacks the ability to dynamically interact with other virtualization entities that may reside in the fabric or on storage arrays. Tighter integration between the host platform and an external virtualization intelligence requires programming interfaces between the two so that the operating system can call upon both internal and external resources to perform specific virtualization services.

In 2001, Microsoft launched multiple initiatives for providing storage APIs to facilitate the creation and modification of virtual storage and to expedite auxiliary services such as snapshots and multiple pathing. These APIs are included in Windows Server 2003, along with software development kits (SDKs) that enable storage vendors to write their own complementary providers. When fully implemented, the direct communication between servers and virtualized storage will allow further automation of repetitive storage administrative tasks in Windows environments.

Microsoft's virtual disk service (VDS), for example, provides a management interface for dynamically creating or dissolving virtual volumes on the fly for specific tasks. Through scripting or a graphical interface, a storage administrator can request a virtualized resource of a desired capacity and RAID level, assign it for a particular application use, and then release it back to the storage pool when the application task is complete. Providing the storage or virtualization vendors have written VDS-compatible interfaces, the request can be fulfilled by any virtualization entity on any storage interconnect.

In effect, the Microsoft VDS virtualizes the control of all other virtualization mechanisms by implementing a vendor-netural, hardware-neutral, and interconnect-netural interface between the operating system and virtual storage. As shown in Figure 6.4, management may be provided by a command line interface (e.g., batch files that are run for a specific task such as backup), a Microsoft graphical interface, or a third-party storage manage-

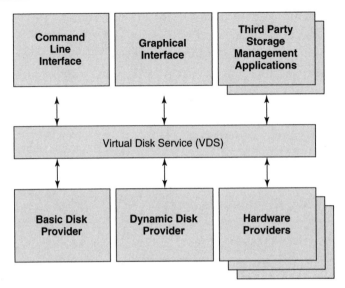

Figure 6.4 Microsoft's virtual disk service (VDS) enables dynamic communication between the operating system and any storage virtualization entity.

ment platform. The virtualization intelligence that communicates with the VDS may reside on the host, in the fabric or on storage systems.

This additional layer of abstraction between upper layer applications and virtual storage systems overcomes potential interoperability problems, but enforcing a common API may prevent administrators from fully leveraging the vendor-proprietary value-added features of some virtualization products. In addition, the vendor and hardware neutrality promoted by VDS applies only to storage, while the Windows operating system itself is inherently proprietary.

Along with VDS, Microsoft is developing auxiliary APIs for snapshots and multi-pathing. The volume shapshot service (VSS) provides APIs for executing nondisruptive volume shadow copies that, in turn, may be written to transient virtualized volumes created by VDS calls. The VSS creates a steady state of a particular volume by temporarily suspending I/O operations and flushing application and operating system buffers. A point-in-time snapshot copy of the volume can then be performed, typically to a virtual disk volume that may be secondarily spooled to tape. VSS code may be integrated into common Microsoft applications such as Exchange and SQL Server to ensure quiessence of the applications for their photo opportunities.

Microsoft's Multipath I/O adds interfaces for identifying and managing multiple paths to the same storage resource. As an enhancement to dual-pathing techniques, Multipath I/O provides up to 32 alternate paths to a storage system and supports both failover of paths as well as load balancing. Although multi-pathing is not a storage virtualization technology, it provides a more robust infrastructure for managing high availability access to virtualized resources.

Collectively, VDS, VSS, Multipath I/O and Microsoft's support for iSCSI and iSNS reflect the steady integration of applications and storage. The virtual disk service further streamlines administration of storage capacity and class of storage by enabling applications to call up virtualized storage assets on demand. Virtual snapshot services enable storage-specific utilities such as point-in-time copying to enforce cooperation by upper layer applications. In addition, the SNIA Storage Management Initiative (SMI-S) is introducing virtualization-enabled services that can be managed through a common standards-based interface. These initiatives may at some point be implemented for Linux or other operating systems and bring us a few steps closer to the ideal of a storage utility.

6.4 Chapter Summary

Logical Volume Management

- 1A logical volume manager (LVM) is a software layer between the file system and the disk driver software of the operating system.

- LVMs can be used to divide large physical disk arrays into more manageable virtual disks or to create large virtual disks from multiple physical disks.

- LVMs may be provided as integral utilities of an operating system or installed as third-party software.

- The functions provided by LVMs are executed by the host CPU.

- LVMs lack hardware-assist for functions such as software RAID/parity generation.

- LVMs provide independence from vendor-specific storage architectures.

- LVMs can provide dynamic capacity allocation to expand or shrink volumes.

- Volume management may support alternate pathing for high availability.

- LVMs are server-centric and must be managed on a per-server basis.

Storage Metadata Servers

- Storage metadata may be shared by multiple servers to facilitate resource sharing.

- Shared storage metadata enables a SAN file system view for multiple servers.

- A storage metadata server provides virtual to real logical block address mapping for client servers.

- Client servers perform I/O across the SAN to storage assets.

- A distributed SAN file system requires file locking mechanisms to preserve data integrity.

Server-Based Storage APIs

- LVMs cannot provide dynamic communication to other virtualization entities.

- Storage-aware APIs may be implemented by the operating system to provide a common interface to disparate virtualization resources.

- Microsoft's virtual disk service (VDS) provides a management interface for dynamic generation of virtualized storage.

- VDS offers on-demand virtual storage capacity and class of storage.

- VDS provides an abstraction layer between the operating system and specific hardware and storage interconnects.

- Volume snapshot service (VSS) coordinates point-in-time copy operations between virtualization engines and upper layer applications.

- VSS may be integrated into Microsoft applications such as Exchange and SQL Server.

- Multi-path I/O facilitates high availability access to virtual storage.

7 Virtualization at the Storage Target

ALTHOUGH SERVER-BASED VIRTUALIZATION offers independence from the unique characteristics of external storage hardware, storage-based virtualization offers independence from the unique characteristics of servers and their operating systems. Vendor-specific attributes of storage systems often provide advanced services and performance advantages that enhance virtualization in homogeneous storage environments. In this chapter, we will examine the options available as virtualization intelligence moves from the server to the storage target.

7.1 Array-Based Virtualization

Storage controllers already provide basic disk virtualization in the form of mirroring and RAID levels. The physical disks under the storage controller's direction can be grouped into LUNs of varying capacities, designated as striped RAID sets for performance and/or data integrity, or assigned as primary and secondary data mirrors. The storage controller typically includes hardware assistance for complex algorithms such as parity generation as well as cache memory to enhance I/O to the servers. In addition, the storage controller may offer a variety of external interfaces, including Fibre Channel, iSCSI, and traditional parallel SCSI ports. Storage systems provide standard block protocol access but present product differentiation through performance, availability, and diagnostic enhancements.

As shown in Figure 7.1, the disk banks in a storage system can be allocated for specific LUN requirements. In this example, four disks provide concatenated storage for LUN 5, while seven disks have been assigned for LUN 2 in a RAID 5 configuration. An equivalent number of disks have been designated for LUN 7, which acts as a mirror to LUN 2. From the

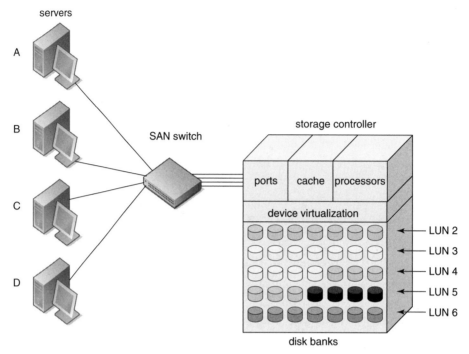

Figure 7.1 RAID controllers for storage arrays provide basic virtualization of the physical disks within the storage cabinet. Block aggregation can be defined for capacity requirements and class of storage.

server perspective, it is writing and reading block data only to LUN 2. The storage controller manages the mirroring algorithm and RAID parity generation for both sets of disks.

Storage controllers can also provide more flexibility in LUN access than server-based virtualization techniques. LUN 3 in the diagram, for example, could be the primary storage allocation for Server A. Servers B through D, however, could also be configured to access LUN 3, with server clustering software managing failover in the event that Server A went off-line.

Because the major providers of storage systems compete on the basis of features, functionality, and price, storage array architectures in the market vary widely in design and execution. Some vendors rely heavily on expensive cache (up to 64 GB) to boost performance, while others may offer minimal cache and depend on massive striping for increased throughput. Some vendors prefer high-end 2 Gbps or 4 Gbps Fibre Channel disks, while others may offer serial ATA (SATA) or serial-attached SCSI (SAS) disk banks. Total storage capacity may range from tens of terabytes to nearly 100 terabytes per storage unit. Some vendors provide redundant processors for failover, as well as advanced diagnostics and phone-home capabilities for proactive maintenance. Most vendors provide LUN masking and LUN mapping to control server access to storage resources. Typically, the greater the functionality, the higher the price. Fortunately for customers, competition continues to drive higher feature/functionality into storage technology, while driving down prices over time. Given that storage systems house the mission-critical data on which enterprises and institutions depend on for their survival, the hardware is a bargain at any price. Reducing management costs of these systems is the current challenge.

If all of a company's business could be run on a single large storage array, device level virtualization alone would be sufficient for managing data storage. Large enterprises, however, may have tens or hundreds of storage systems, and although these may be configured on storage networks, management of multiple systems requires significant administrative overhead. As in direct-attached storage, increasing quantity may result in decreasing quality, as the higher population of storage systems contributes to inefficient utilization of storage capacity and inability to easily share dispersed storage assets between applications. In addition, even a resilient storage system cannot guarantee continuous data access. The failure of the entire array or disruption to the data center housing it threatens data availability. Coordination of assets between multiple storage systems is therefore necessary to ensure continuous data access, efficient storage utilization, and simplified management.

For array-based virtualization to graduate from management of discrete disks within a cabinet to the virtualization of entire storage systems, additional intelligence is required. As shown in Figure 7.2, communication between separate storage controllers enables the disk resources of each system to be managed collectively, either through a distributed management scheme or through a hierarchal master/slave relationship. The communication protocol between storage subsystems may be proprietary or based on the SNIA SMI-S standard. A proprietary implementation may be beneficial, however, since although it precludes interoperability with other vendor's storage arrays, it tends to maximize the value-add of the specific vendor's storage architecture. Customers who are content with homogeneous storage may get higher functionality and better performance from a system virtualization solution than if an open system mechanism was used.

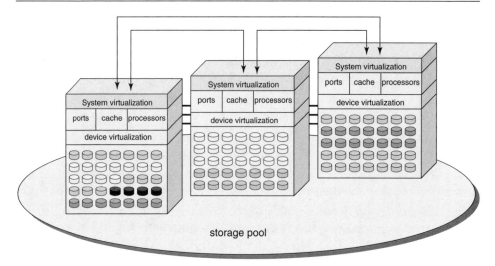

Figure 7.2 Coordination of assets between storage arrays requires system-level virtualization intelligence to facilitate storage pooling.

Virtualization at the storage target creates a new abstraction layer above device-level abstraction and the presentation of storage to servers. From the standpoint of the server, nothing has changed. It continues to access data via LUNs that, in the case of storage networking, are associated with network addresses. With a single storage array, the LUNs are supported by disk assets within a single chassis. In system-level virtualization, the LUNs may be supported by disks dispersed over multiple arrays either within the data center or between geographically remote sites.

7.2 Array-Based Data Replication

As one of the first forms of array-to-array virtualization, data replication requires that a storage system function as a target to its attached servers and as an initiator to a secondary array. Commonly referred to as disk-to-disk (D2D) data replication, this functionality is generally available as an option on all major storage systems. EMC's Symmetrix Remote Data Facility (SRDF) for its high-end arrays, EMC MirrorView for CLARiiON midrange systems, EMC SAN Copy between CLARiiON and Symmetrix (or third-party arrays), IBM Peer to Peer Remote Copy (PPRC) for Shark arrays, HDS TrueCopy for the Thunder and Lightning series arrays, HP Data Replication Manager (DRM) for StorageWorks systems, Xiotech REDI

SANlinks for Magnitude arrays, Compellent Remote Instant Replay for Storage Center systems, and other utilities all provide array-to-array communication for mirroring data from one system to another.

Array-based data replication may be synchronous or asynchronous, depending on the recovery point objective requirements. In a synchronous replication operation as shown in Figure 7.3, each write to a primary array must be completed on the secondary array before the SCSI transaction acknowledges completion. The SCSI I/O is therefore dependent on speed at which both writes can be performed, and any latency between the two systems affects overall performance. For this reason, synchronous data replication is generally limited to metropolitan distances (~150 kilometers) to avoid performance degradation due to speed of light propagation delay.

In asynchronous array-based replication, individual write operations to the primary array are acknowledged locally, while one or more write transactions may be queued to the secondary array as shown in Figure 7.4. This

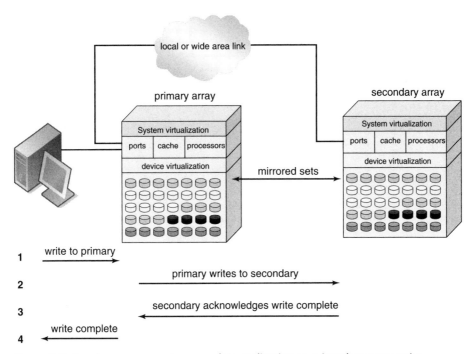

Figure 7.3 Synchronous array-to-array data replication requires that every write transaction must be completed at the secondary array before it is acknowledged by the primary.

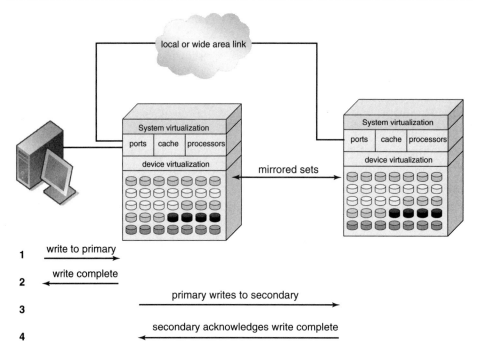

Figure 7.4 Asynchronous array-to-array data replication improves performance through local acknowledgement, but cannot guarantee that the most current transaction has been secured on the secondary array.

solves the problem of local performance, but may result in loss of the most current writes to the secondary array if the link between the two systems is lost. To minimize this risk, some implementations required the primary array to temporarily buffer each pending transaction to the secondary so that transient disruptions are recoverable. Asynchronous data replication is largely immune to speed of light latency and so can be extended over thousands of kilometers, but it exposes the primary site to loss of the buffered data in the event of a failure of the primary array.

Because asynchronous replication confirms write completion before the data is actually copied at the secondary array, there is always a disparity between data on the two systems. This disparity is compounded when the primary system buffers multiple I/Os on a regular interval before sending them as a batch update to the secondary array. A server, for example, may update a banking record several times during a buffer interval, and the primary would send the updates en masse and possibly out of order to the secondary storage array. Time-stamping each buffered transaction enables the primary array to only send the most current record update, ensure in-order delivery of writes, and thus maintain data consistency between the two systems.

Synchronous data replication provides the highest level of data consistency but is fairly limited in terms of distance. Asynchronous replication breaks the distance barrier, but at the expense of data consistency between primary and secondary arrays. The most common storage application for both implementations is disaster recovery, and consequently the desired recovery time objective (RTO) and recovery point objective (RPO) will generally dictate which replication method is used. The recovery time objective may vary from one type of business to another. Retail businesses, for example, may be able to withstand a data outage for some time as long as regional stores are still open and customers continue to make purchases. Financial institutions, by contrast, may lose tens of millions of dollars for every hour of downtime. The recovery point objective, likewise, may vary from one business to another, but most enterprises would like to have access to the very latest transaction that occurred before an outage.

The narrow circumference of ~150 kilometers provided by synchronous replication is, sadly, no longer sufficient to provide a safe haven for replicated data. Financial institutions in New York, for example, that previously replicated from Manhattan to New Jersey, are now attempting to secure disaster recovery capabilities well outside the vulnerable East Coast region. Because it is not possible to drive synchronous replication further than a few hundred miles, new disaster recovery strategies are combining synchronous and asynchronous replication methods. Synchronous replication may be implemented within a region to ensure that the very latest transaction is captured at the disaster recovery site, and asynchronous replication installed between the disaster recovery site and a third site well beyond regional exposure (e.g., New York to New Jersey synchronous; New Jersey to Colorado Springs asynchronous). This is an expensive solution, but an essential one to provide maximum recoverability in the event of major disruptions.

Array-based data replication is transparent to the host systems whose data it protects. The backend complexities of synchronization of primary and secondary (and possibly tertiary) volumes, consistency management, error handling, and recovery are virtualized as a simple transaction between initiators and their assigned LUNs on the primary array. Configuring array-based replication, however, is no quite so straightforward. In addition to the array-specific parameters, the links between arrays and their associated wide-area hardware components require substantial management during installation. Some storage systems come preconfigured for storage pools of different types to facilitate installation. Typically, once data replication solutions are put in place, recurring management overhead is minimal.

7.3 Array-Based Point-in-Time Copy (Snapshot)

Array-based virtualization services often include automated point-in-time copies or snapshots that may be implemented as a complement to data replication. Synchronous and asynchronous data replication captures data changes on a per-write basis. Snapshots periodically capture data changes of an entire volume, regardless of how many individual writes have occurred. Because data replication is monitoring discrete modifications to data blocks, it assumes that the application-generated write requests have exited the application and operating system buffers. In reality, there may still be pending write operations held in cache at any given moment. To ensure an accurate point-in-time copy of data, snapshot technology must have some means to interact with the applications and operating system to ensure that buffers have been flushed, pending transactions have been sent to the array, and the snapshot accurately reflects the point-in-time state of all application data. This type of capability is defined in the SNIA SMI-S copy services profile.

A snapshot utility may be implemented within a single array chassis, with disks assigned for snapshot retention. If the entire array fails, however, the original volume and its snapshots would be unavailable. For high availability, array-based snapshots may be created on a secondary array (or multiple arrays) at predetermined intervals, as shown in Figure 7.5. In this example, volume snapshots are taken every two hours. In most implementations, it is not necessary to copy the entire volume for each snapshot. If the intervening writes are logged and synchronized between copies, only the changed data needs to be copied (e.g., copy on write or COW). This adds complexity to the snapshot operation, but reduces the amount of data transfer between primary and secondary arrays.

A key advantage of array-based snapshots is the ability to quickly restore a volume to a known good state. If, for instance, an Exchange server is exposed to a debilitating virus, the previous virus-free snapshot can be restored to resume operations with minimal data loss. Because this restoration may in some implementations occur directly between the disk arrays

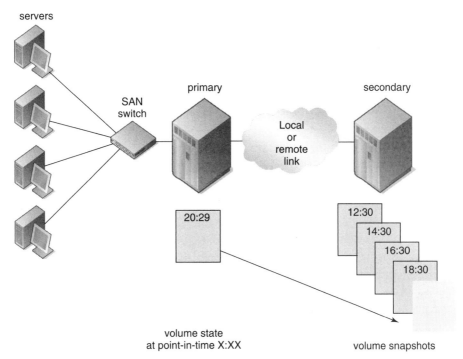

Figure 7.5 A primary array may create point-in-time snapshots that are stored on a secondary array. In the event of data corruption or loss, a known good state of a volume can be restored.

themselves, data transfer is direct and far more efficient than data restoration from tape or via a third-party appliance.

7.4 Distributed Modular Array Virtualization

Following the precedent set by NAS vendors, storage array providers have begun to decouple the storage controller intelligence from the disk assets they manage. First-generation NAS products were marketed as monolithic units that housed both file serving logic and disk arrays. The current trend, however, is toward NAS "heads" that separate the file serving intelligence from disk assets. This solution provides greater flexibility for connecting disk resources and accommodating a greater diversity of disk types (Fibre Channel, SATA, SAS, etc.). Separating block storage controller logic from disk resources provides the same flexibility and enables distribution of virtualization services over a more resilient storage cluster.

Traditional storage array architecture binds the storage controller to its disk banks, typically within a single large chassis and adjacent chassis that are bolted together in one extended unit. There are many advantages to this architecture, including ease of maintenance, redundant power, cooling, and shortest path between the storage controller and disks. It has proven less flexible, though, in allowing customers to provision different generations of disks or more economical disk types and in providing alternate protocols such as iSCSI for block data access.

As storage controllers acquire advanced services through storage virtualization and are able to coordinate tasks between their peers, it is logical to wean storage virtualizers from their local disk enclosures. Clustering storage controllers satisfies high availability requirements through cluster failover mechanisms and enables load balancing between controller systems. In addition, greater flexibility in supporting a diversity of disk assets allows a distributed system to more easily implement class of storage services and data lifecycle management.

The diagram in Figure 7.6 shows a storage cluster of three controllers managing Fibre Channel, SATA, SAS, and SCSI disk banks. The controllers

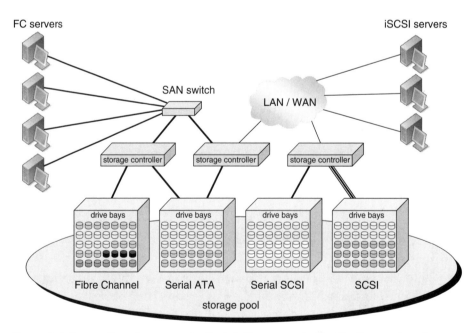

Figure 7.6 Decoupling storage controller intelligence and virtualization engines from physical disk banks facilitates multi-protocol block data access and accommodation of a broad range of disk architectures.

jointly manage a heterogeneous storage pool, enabling, for example, the use of economical serial ATA disks as secondary mirrors to more expensive Fibre Channel disks. Performance is a potential issue once the controller and disk banks are no longer collocated in the same chassis, but new clock rates for Fibre Channel at 4 Gbps and 10 Gbps, as well as 10 Gbps Ethernet may provide adequate throughput. The clear advantage of a distributed storage controller architecture is in its ability to accommodate the trend toward more flexible storage allocation with heterogeneous disk assets and access protocols. This is still a proprietary configuration, however, since the controllers and their detached disk assets are vendor-specific.

Figure 7.6 also reveals another trend, however. By decoupling storage controller and virtualization intelligence from physical disk assets, the traditional functionality of storage controllers now appears as a network capability instead of an integral storage array capability. If a box on the network now supports RAID management, LUN creation and assignment, communication between other intelligent entities, data replication, snapshots, and other virtualization services, then the box could as easily incorporate the functions of fabric switching. One less box in the diagram. What is occurring in the market, though, is that the SAN switch is capable of assuming the functionality of the storage controller, including distributed virtualization services and failover capability.

7.5 Chapter Summary

Array-Based Virtualization

- Storage controllers provide basic disk virtualization in the form of RAID management, mirroring, and LUN mapping/masking.

- Storage controllers may offer Fibre Channel, iSCSI, and SCSI protocols for block storage access.

- For enterprise-class storage arrays, Fibre Channel disk banks are typically used.

- Storage controllers may allocate a single LUN to multiple servers for applications such as server clustering.

- Storage arrays may include cache memory for enhanced performance.

- Coordination of storage assets between multiple storage systems is necessary to ensure high availability.

- There is no open systems standard for peer communication between storage arrays.

- System-level array-based virtualization enables storage controllers to coordinate block data functions between multiple arrays.

Array-Based Data Replication

- Array-based data replication is commonly referred to as disk-to-disk replication.

- Array-based data replication requires that a storage controller function concurrently as both an initiator and target.

- Synchronous data replication ensures that a write operation to a secondary disk array is completed before the primary array acknowledges task completion to the server.

- To preserve performance, synchronous data replication is typically limited to metropolitan distances.

- Asynchronous data replication provides write completion by the primary array, although the transaction may still be pending to the secondary array.

- Asynchronous data replication is largely immune to transmission latency.

- Time stamping of write transactions may be used to ensure in-order delivery of buffered writes for asynchronous replication.

- Synchronous and asynchronous array-based data replication may be combined to provide maximum recoverability of current data.

Array-Based Point-in-Time Copy (Snapshot)

- An intelligent storage controller may provide point-in-time copies of an entire storage volume.

- For high availability, snapshot copies may be written to secondary storage arrays.

- Logging block changes between snapshots (copy on write) enables an image of the original to be maintained without duplicating the data.

- Array-based snapshots provide an efficient means to quickly recover a known good volume state in the event of data from the host.

Distributed Modular Array Virtualization

- Decoupling storage controller logic from physical disk banks provides flexibility for supporting heterogeneous disk assets and facilitates distributed virtualization intelligence.

- Distributed array-based virtualization accommodates class of storage services and data lifecycle management.

- The separation of array controller logic from disk enclosures promotes array-based virtualization as a network-based capability.

8

Fabric-Based Virtualization

A FABRIC IS A SWITCHED INFRASTRUCTURE designed for high-speed data transport. In SAN environments, a fabric provides both high performance transfer of block storage data and auxiliary services to streamline network addressing, device discovery, and notification of changes to the fabric. In this chapter we examine the additional fabric-based services for virtualization of storage resources within the storage network itself.

8.1 Sentient SANs

Traditional data communication networks provide connectivity between computer platforms and are optimized for efficient data transport from source to destination. Based predominantly on Ethernet and TCP/IP protocols, these networks are commonly referred to as messaging networks since the vast majority of data traffic is in the form of discrete files or records exchanged between sender and receiver. Email, web pages, online order entry updates, and so on constantly transit the public Internet and private intranets across conventional IP-routed networks. Although messaging networks may provide some auxiliary services such as domain name service (DNS) and dynamic host configuration protocol (DHCP), the network infrastructure generally relies on the intelligence of the end systems to establish and maintain coherent end-to-end conversations. In a traditional network, all end devices are initiators. If you type an Internet address into your browser, for example, the network will provide the connection to your destination. The assumption, however, is that you knew where you wanted to go and could initiate the transaction.

A storage area network cannot assume that an end device is particularly intelligent. A SAN-attached device may, in fact, be relatively challenged, as in the case of a JBOD that lacks RAID controller logic to act on its collective behalf. The basic division between SAN initiators, such as servers, and SAN targets, such as storage arrays and tape subsystems, reflects the active and passive roles of SAN participants. Targets do not initiate transactions, but wait passively for an initiator to establish a storage session with them. Initiators actively pursue connectivity with targets, but must first know where those targets reside. A storage network must therefore provide a means for targets to register their presence on the SAN and for initiators to be given the appropriate network addresses of their assigned targets. In short, the network itself must be intelligent to accommodate the disparity between its active and passive end devices.

Unlike conventional Ethernet switches that simply transfer data from port to port, a fabric switch in a SAN must additionally provide device logon services, name server registration, and change notification for its clients. Although a Fibre Channel device has a 64-bit unique World Wide Name (WWN), it has no network address when it initially connects to the fabric. It must first log on to the fabric and acquire a unique 3-byte fabric address for network communication. It then registers its attributes with a simple name server (SNS) database maintained by the fabric switch. Additionally, the device may register with the registered state change notification (RSCN) entity within the fabric so that it can be proactively notified of the entry or exit of devices from the fabric.

After having logged onto and registered with the fabric, an initiator will query the SNS to discover the network addresses of its intended targets. Once the fabric responds with a list of target addresses, the initiator can then do what it originally intended to do: access storage data via the SAN. Additional intelligence in the fabric in the form of zoning, LUN masking and LUN mapping can be used to control the target resources that are made visible to initiators through the SNS query mechanism.

In addition to logon, SNS, and RSCN services, fabrics were designed to be self-configuring. Switch-to-switch protocols as defined in ANSI FC-SW-2 govern fabric-building when two or more switches are connected through expansion (E_Port) ports. Fabric-building protocols are meant to ensure that each fabric switch has a unique block of 64k addresses that can be allocated to switch ports and assigned to attached end devices. This avoids potential address duplication in the fabric and misrouting of data. In addition, switches in a multi-switch fabric may exchange SNS data and zoning set information so that devices on one side of the fabric can discover authorized resources on the other side. Switch-to-switch protocols are also used to determine connectivity paths through the fabric using the fabric shortest path first (FSPF) protocol.

This suite of device and fabric-building services is supported by microcode and processing power within every switch in a fabric. Ethernet switches, by contrast, may support virtual LANs (VLANs, analogous to zoning) and open shortest path first (OSPF, from which FSPF was developed), but they do not provide logon services, address assignment, name servers, device discovery, change notification, or storage-specific features such as LUN masking or LUN mapping. Although it is tempting to compare the per-port pricing of Ethernet switches to their Fibre Channel brethren, the additional intelligence provided by fabric switches will inevitably impose a premium even as fabric switch prices continue to decline.

Because fabrics already supply advanced services to convenience storage transactions and are the nexus of all relationships between servers and storage, they are a likely candidate for network-based storage virtualization, security, and other storage enhancements in the network. Where server-based virtualization provides independence from vendor-specific storage, and storage-based virtualization provides independence from vendor-specific servers and operating systems, fabric-based virtualization provides independence from both. The fabric is, after all, already providing connectivity to heterogeneous server platforms and heterogeneous storage arrays and tape subsystems. A single fabric switch, for example, may provide connections to Solaris, Windows, AIX, and Linux servers as well as EMC, IBM, HDS, and HP storage. As shown in Figure 8.1, because all storage traffic must pass through the fabric, the fabric has the opportunity to intervene in storage transactions, manipulate network address and LUN parameters, maintain logical block address maps for virtual LUNs, recalculate frame CRCs (cyclic redundancy checks), and so on, independently of the vendor-specific attributes of storage or server platforms.

Fabric-based virtualization represents a further evolutionary step toward network-based intelligence, but it is a step that requires considerable deliberation. The fabric is already tasked with multi-gigabit transport, discovery, zoning, routing, and network-building responsibilities. As with other virtualization strategies, fabric-based virtualization must not only provide facilities for storage pooling and auxiliary services such as data

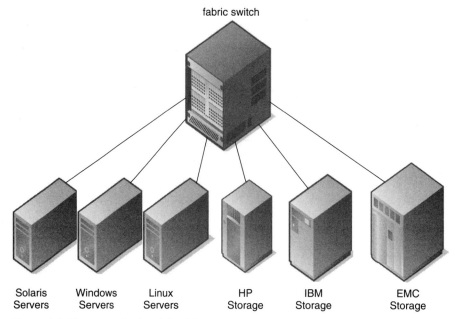

fabric switch

Solaris   Windows   Linux   HP   IBM   EMC
Servers   Servers   Servers   Storage   Storage   Storage

Figure 8.1 The central role of the fabric in providing connectivity for heterogeneous storage assets and servers positions is to intervene in storage transactions and provide advanced virtualization services.

replication and snapshots, but also be capable of handling potential back-end disruptions and errors. In addition, because a fabric may be composed of multiple switches from different vendors, the assumption of virtualization capabilities may require standardized protocols to ensure interoperability between fabric-hosted virtualization engines.

Virtualization intelligence in the fabric does not preclude intelligence on storage end systems or hosts, i.e., an intelligent fabric switch may facilitate storage virtualization by dynamically interacting with virtualizers on arrays, servers, or appliances. This would enable, for example, fabric-based virtualization to handle some general pooling functions while letting RAID controllers perform more problematic distributed array-based virtualization functions or letting server-based virtualization coordinate failover mechanisms. Industry observers and competing storage vendors may disagree about how much intelligence should be entrusted to the network, but the centrality of the storage network infrastructure is too pivotal to be left to simple frame switching.

8.2 Techniques for Switch-Based Virtualization

As in array-based storage virtualization, fabric-based virtualization requires additional processing power and memory on top of a hardware architecture that is concurrently providing processing power for fabric services, switching, and other tasks. Because large fabric switches (directors) are typically built on a chassis and option blade or line card scheme, virtualization capability is being introduced as yet another blade that slots into the director chassis, as shown in Figure 8.2. This provides the advantage of tighter integration with the port cards that service storage and servers but consumes expensive director real estate for slot that could otherwise support additional end devices. If a virtualization blade is not properly engineered, it may degrade the overall availability specification of the director. A five-nines (99.999%) available director will inevitably lose some nines if a marginal option card is introduced.

Because software virtualization products have been around for some time, it is tempting to simply host one or another of those applications on a fabric switch. Typically, software virtualization runs on Windows or Linux, which in turn implies that a virtualization blade that hosts software will

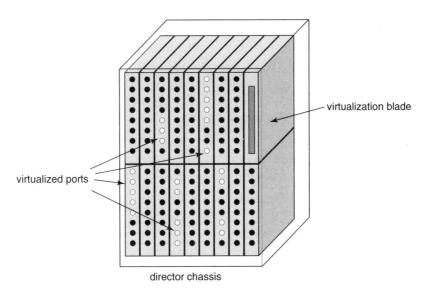

virtualization blade

virtualized ports

director chassis

Figure 8.2 A storage virtualization engine as an option card within a director should enable virtualization of any storage asset on any director port.

essentially be a PC on a card. This design has the advantage, for the vendor at least, of time to market, but as with host or appliance virtualization products in general, it may pose potential performance issues if the PC logic cannot cope with high traffic volumes. Consequently, some vendors are pursuing hardware-assisted virtualization on fabric switches by creating ASICs (application specific integrated circuits) that are optimized for high-performance frame decoding and block address mapping. These ASICs may be implemented on director blades or on auxiliary modules mounted in the director enclosure.

Whether the fabric-based virtualization engine is hosted on a PC blade, an optimized ASIC blade or auxiliary module, it should have the flexibility to provide virtualization services to any port on the director. In a standard fabric architecture, frames are simply switched from one port to another based on destination Fibre Channel address. Depending on the virtualization method used, the fabric virtualization engine may intervene in this process by redirecting frames from various ports according to the requirements of the virtual logical address mapping of a virtualized LUN. In addition, if a storage asset is moved from one physical port to another, the virtualization engine must monitor the change in network address to preserve consistent device mapping. This adds considerable complexity to internal fabric management to accommodate the adds, moves, and changes that are inevitable in storage networking.

Given the high availability requirements of enterprise SANs, fabric-based virtualization should also provide for failover between virtualization engines, both for redundant blades within a single chassis and between switches. This requires a heartbeat or load-balancing mechanism and distribution of logical block address maps so that every virtualization engine has the current status of virtualized storage assets. Synchronization between virtualization entities distributed throughout a complex fabric may be more challenging for vendors, but it will become a customer requirement to ensure high availability in the event of a particular switch or virtualization engine failure. In addition, as fabric-based virtualization solutions become more widespread, interoperability between different vendor implementations will become a priority. Fortunately, steps are already being taken to facilitate multi-vendor fabric virtualization, as we will see in the following section on the fabric application interface standard (FAIS) initiative.

8.3 The Fabric Application Interface Standard (FAIS)

FAIS is an open systems project of the ANSI/INCITS T11.5 task group and defines a set of common APIs to be implemented within fabrics. The APIs are a means to more easily integrate storage applications that were originally developed as host, array, or appliance-based utilities to now be supported within fabric switches and directors. FAIS development is thus being driven by the switch manufacturers as well as by companies who have developed storage virtualization software and virtualization hardware-assist components.

Because fabric switches connect servers to storage and may be configured to provide primary, alternate, or load-balancing paths to storage array ports, embedding storage virtualization within switches offers the additional advantage of manipulating data paths within the fabric to better service storage I/Os. In a distributed FAIS implementation, it would therefore be possible for a multi-switch fabric to constantly optimize complex data pathing between switches to accelerate performance while maintaining high availability storage access.

The FAIS initiative separates control information from the data path. In practice, this division of labor is implemented as two different types of processors, as shown in Figure 8.3. The control path processor (CPP) supports some form of operating system, the FAIS application interface, and the storage virtualization application. The CPP is therefore a high-performance CPU with auxiliary memory, centralized within the switch architecture. It supports multiple instances of SCSI initiator and SCSI target modes and, via the supported storage virtualization application, presents the virtualized view of storage to the servers. Allocation of virtualized storage to individual servers and management of the storage metadata is the responsibility of the storage application running on the CPP.

The data path controller (DPC) may be implemented at the port level in the form of an ASIC or dedicated CPU. The DPC is optimized for low latency and high bandwidth to execute basic SCSI read/write transactions under the management of one or more CPPs. Mirroring, for example, may be performed by a DPC, but the DPC relies on control information from the CPP to define where the mirroring should be done.

The FAIS specifications do not define a particular hardware design for CPP and DPC entities, so vendor implementation may vary considerably

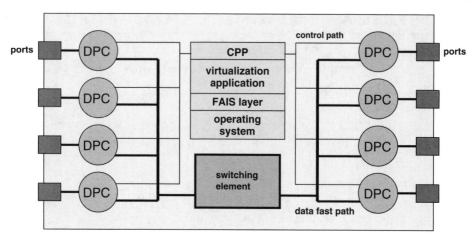

Figure 8.3 FAIS divides control and data into separate paths and processing units. The control path processor (CPP) supports the virtualization software while off-loading some virtualization tasks to port-based data path controllers (DPCs).

from one brand of switch to another. As long as the basic functionality is uniform, it should be possible to build distributed FAIS environments across multi-vendor fabrics. The general objective of the FAIS initiative is to provide fabric-based services such as snapshots, mirroring, and data replication while maintaining high-performance switching of storage data. The fact that the storage data may reside on highly virtualized physical assets should be completely transparent to the user.

Although FAIS is being developed in a standards body task group traditionally focused on Fibre Channel, FAIS is meant to accommodate iSCSI storage data as well. The diagram in Figure 8.3 therefore does not indicate what type of transport protocol is used. The separation of control and data paths and hosting of virtualization applications via APIs is not specific to Fibre Channel, but aligns with other intelligent services offered by Fibre Channel fabric switches. In an iSCSI environment, similar virtualization functionality would have to be hosted in a network switch or router optimized for IP storage transactions. This of course opens new market opportunities for IP network equipment manufacturers, just as IP storage in general is bringing new high volume traffic to traditional LANs and WANs.

FAIS is predicated on a tight integration of virtualization services with high-performance switching and pathing. The virtualization application resident on the switch must be able to identify and query storage assets that are potential targets for virtualizing. It must also be able to query the fabric to discover what data paths are available between servers and storage arrays. Having identified assets and paths, however, is only half the job. To be useful and maintain the illusion of simplicity, the virtualization application must be able to deal with exceptions, both for the virtualized SCSI transactions and for potential faults along the data path. The link state of a particular path, for example, must be monitored so that I/Os can be directed along alternate paths if necessary. Because the DPC is optimized for high performance switching and basic virtualized SCSI read/write operations, it will call on the CPP to respond to fault conditions. The requirement to rapidly respond to exceptions drives complexity into fabric-based virtualization, particularly as distributed FAIS-enabled solutions are developed.

As with other standards documents, FAIS draft specifications owe their succinctness to heavy reliance on acronyms whose meanings are crystal clear to the authors but undecipherable to the general citizenry. Two key acronyms are BITL and FITL. To clarify, BITL is Back I_T_L_Nexus and FITL is Front I_T_L_Nexus. I_T_L, in turn, is an identifying tuple for the FAIS initiator port ID (to which a server is attached), the FAIS target port ID (to which storage assets are attached), and a logical unit number (LUN). The I_T_L designation satisfies SCSI standards requirements for defining associations between initiator and targets: one SCSI initiator – one SCSI target – one logical unit within the target. The FITL in this case has one real component (the initiator ID) and two virtualized components (the target ID and LUN). Because the presentation of a target and LUN to the initiator is a fabrication of the virtualization application, there is no direct association between the initiator and actual target/LUN identifiers on the backend fabric storage connections. That association is provided by the BITL, which identifies real paths to underlying storage assets that are used to generate the virtualized volume.

As shown in Figure 8.4, each server connection is assigned an initiator ID that typically represents a single HBA attachment to the fabric. From the server's standpoint, it sees a storage volume that in reality is being virtualized within the switch. This is the frontend view, represented by ITL 1 and ITL 2. On the backend storage side, each actual target connection that composes a virtualized volume are identified by a target ID and associated LUN, as shown by ITL 3 and ITL 4.

Because access to a single physical target may be provided by multiple paths (BITLs), these paths are listed as part of a BITL_Set. These paths may be active/passive for some storage arrays or allow concurrent access for

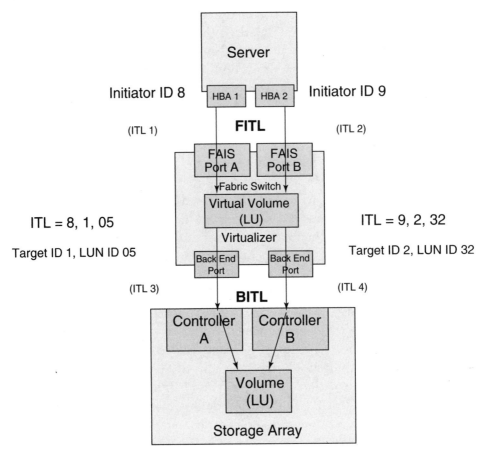

Figure 8.4 FAIS provides an initiator, target, and LUN (ITL) identifier to specify server access to virtualized storage resources and fabric connectivity to underlying storage resources.

load balancing in others. Paths are weighted within the BITL_Set object so that the DPC can select the appropriate path or paths for I/O execution.

The virtual volumes served up by the fabric switch are identified as virtual devices, or VDEVs. A virtual device may be composed of multiple block ranges distributed over several physical storage arrays, whose assets are identified by the BITL_Set, or composed of other virtual devices.

As shown in Figure 8.5, virtual device 1 (VDEV1) is a virtualized storage asset supported by mirroring in virtual devices VDEV2 and VDEV3. VDEV2, in this case, is composed of two additional virtual devices, VDEV4 and VDEV5. VDEV4 and VDEV5 are assigned logical block address ranges from separate physical storage arrays, represented by their respective

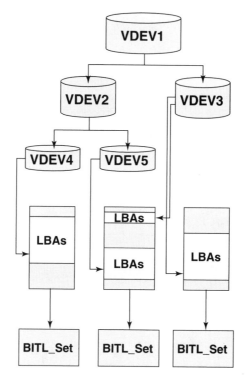

Figure 8.5 Virtual devices (VDEVs) may
be composed of other virtual devices or
designated block ranges accessible via
backend storage paths.

BITL_Sets. The mirror for VDEV1 is VDEV3, which concatenates logical
block address ranges from two different BITL_Sets.

The ability to use virtual devices as building blocks for larger virtual devices provides a highly flexible means to dynamically size virtualized storage capacity and implement combinations of mirroring and block striping
for reliability and performance. The virtualization application is responsible
for creating these virtualized structures, and then uses FAIS API calls to
download mapping information to the DPCs. Once activated on a DPC, the
DPC references the BITL_Set to determine optimum pathing to the physical
storage assets and executes mirroring, striping, data replication, or snapshots as defined under CPP control.

During operation, monitoring the status of virtual device regions is performed by the XMAP object. Access, read/write permissions to the virtual
volume, and monitoring of I/Os in progress to different portions of a VDEV

help ensure data integrity and correct handling of exceptions that need to be passed to the CPP for resolution.

Because Fibre Channel initiators discover their storage targets by querying the fabric's simple name server, storage resources virtualized via FAIS must be registered as conventional storage devices. In addition, standard fabric zoning may be used to restrict the visibility of virtualized storage to designated servers. The cohabitation of traditional fabric services and fabric-based virtualization services should facilitate integration of these functions and simplify management through a common interface.

8.4 Chapter Summary

Sentient SANs

- A storage network requires intelligent services to compensate for the passive nature of networked storage targets.

- The Fibre Channel architecture provides logon services, a simple name server, change notification, fabric building, network address assignment, zoning, and LUN masking/mapping to convenience storage transactions.

- Fabric-based virtualization represents an extension of fabric-based intelligent services.

- A fabric switch provides connectivity for all storage transactions and interoperability between disparate servers, operating systems, and target devices.

- Fabric-based virtualization may interface with other virtualization entities on hosts, arrays, or appliances.

Techniques for Switch-Based Virtualization

- Fabric-based virtualization may be hosted on departmental switches or data center directors.

- Director-based virtualization engines should be able to preserve the five nines availability characteristic of director-class switches.

- Fabric-based virtualization may be hosted on a PC engine provisioned as an option blade.

- Dedicated virtualization ASICs provide high-performance frame processing and block address mapping.

- High availability may be provided by distributed fabric-based virtualization with synchronization of virtual mapping between intelligent switches.

Fabric Application Interface Standard (FAIS)
- FAIS is a project of the ANSI/INCITS T11.5 task group.

- FAIS defines a set of standard APIs to integrate storage applications and SAN switches.

- FAIS separates control information and data paths.

- The control path processor (CPP) supports the FAIS APIs and upper layer storage virtualization application.

- The data path controller (DPC) executes the virtualized SCSI I/Os under the management of one or more CPPs.

- The Front I_T_L_Nexus (FITL) identifies the connectivity between a server and the fabric-based virtualization entity.

- The Back I_T_L_Nexus (BITL) identifies the connectivity between the fabric-based virtualization engine and underlying storage targets.

- A BITL_Set defines multiple paths available to storage for failover or load balancing.

- A VDEV is a virtual device configured by the virtualization application.

- A VDEV may be composed of secondary VDEVs.

- Virtual storage mapping defined by the CPP is downloaded to the DPC for execution.

- Based on VDEV assignments, the DPC may perform mirroring, striping, data replication, or snapshot operations.

- The XMAP object monitors access, permissions, and I/O status of a VDEV and calls the CPP for exception handling.

- The integration of traditional fabric services with FAIS and fabric-based virtualization should simplify management of both storage transport and storage placement.

9

Virtualization Appliances

LIKE FABRIC-BASED VIRTUALIZATION, virtualization appliances may provide independence from both host systems and storage targets, readily lending themselves to heterogeneous, multi-vendor environments. In some implementations, however, appliances rely on supporting software on each server. This chapter examines the functionality and options available for appliance-based virtualization, as well as advantages it may provide compared to other solutions.

9.1 Black Box Virtualization

Among the first system-level virtualization products, storage virtualization appliances offer yet another means to pool storage assets and automate data replication, snapshot, and other storage operations. The term *appliance* implies a plug-and-play capability that for virtualization products is still under construction. Performing initial system setup and definition of virtual volumes still requires careful planning and attention to configuration details. An appliance also conveys the notion of a third-party add-on solution, a specialized black box that attaches to an established network to provide auxiliary functions between heterogeneous end devices. As with fabric-based virtualization, one of the strengths of an appliance approach is the ability to accommodate a wide variety of operating systems, host platforms, and storage targets.

Analogous to NAS appliances, virtualization appliances may be marketed as hardware platforms that run a thin, optimized operating system and software and provide a variety of interconnects for attaching to SCSI, Fibre Channel, or iSCSI environments. Alternately, some vendors provide virtualization software that runs on any standard Wintel processor and leave it to the customer to select the PC platform, memory, and interface cards appropriate for their environment. In either case, the appliance is attached to the network as a peer end device or inserted in line between storage and servers. Appliance architectures vary considerably from vendor to vendor. Some products are positioned for enterprise data centers, and thus assume connectivity to existing Fibre Channel SANs. Other products are engineered for medium and small businesses and emphasize connectivity to conventional SCSI storage devices or some mix of parallel SCSI and modular Fibre Channel arrays. Likewise, host block access via the appliance may be supported on a variety of protocols, including Fibre Channel, iSCSI, or proprietary IP protocols.

The early development of storage virtualization appliances spawned vigorous religious disputes over the value of in-band (a.k.a. symmetric) and out-of-band (a.k.a. asymmetric) approaches to storage virtualization. Unfortunately, the jihad waged by opposing vendor camps has contributed to the confusion over storage virtualization and often obscured its practical end-user value in simplifying storage management.

9.2 In-Band Virtualization Appliances

Storage virtualization is predicated on control information about where virtualized data storage actually exists and the transport of the actual data itself to and from virtualized storage. In a networked environment, this duality equates to a control path for the storage metadata and a data path for retrieval from or commitment to data to disk. In-band storage virtualization sends control information in the form of metadata along the same path as the data transport and thus positions the virtualization appliance directly between servers and storage. In-line or in-band virtualization may be implemented in a number of ways, depending on the type of storage targets and block access protocols used.

For Fibre Channel environments, in-band virtualization may split the storage network into two separate fabrics: one for host connectivity to the appliance and another for appliance connectivity to storage targets. As shown in Figure 9.1, server platforms have no direct access to physical storage arrays but communicate solely through the virtualization appliance. In this example, the virtualization appliance appears as a storage target to the fabric switch connecting the servers, presenting target IDs and virtualized LUNs to the fabric. This enables the storage appliance to leverage the fab-

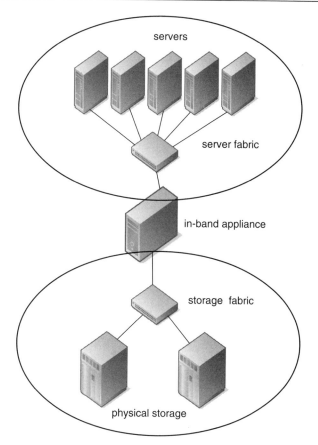

Figure 9.1 An in-band storage virtualization appliance may sit directly between separate Fibre Channel fabrics to physically segregate servers from the storage targets.

ric's zoning utility to manage visibility of the LUNs and provide high performance access between the server platforms and the appliance.

For the physical storage devices on the storage fabric, the appliance appears as an initiator, proxying multiple SCSI client sessions on behalf of the actual but isolated servers. In this case, the appliance behaves as a typical Fibre Channel initiator, querying the fabric's simple name server for resources. Once it has identified and established sessions with individual disk arrays via the fabric, however, the appliance can perform LUN manipulation to create storage pools and build storage metadata for mapping physical assets to virtualized ones.

The in-band approach may also be applied to Ethernet-attached hosts as shown in Figure 9.2. Block storage access over Ethernet is accomplished using iSCSI or vendor-specific IP block protocols, while back-end storage access may be through Fibre Channel, parallel SCSI, SATA, or other disk protocols. Some in-band virtualization appliances provide an entry-level IP SAN for small businesses, using iSCSI device drivers at zero cost for servers and pooling of legacy parallel SCSI devices for virtual storage.

Some in-band appliance solutions may require host-resident software drivers, particularly when proprietary transport protocols are used. Control metadata may be split between the server clients and the appliance, with the appliance exporting current block mapping data to the servers. In this case, the control path is also the data path, since there is only one physical conduit between a server and the appliance to pass both metadata and data. Alternately, all control information may be resident within the appliance, which simply offers virtualized LUNs to servers and handles logical address block mapping internally.

As shown in these graphical examples, the obvious concern about in-band virtualization is that the appliance itself will become a bottleneck for storage transactions, particularly as the traffic load from multiple servers increases. Vendors have tried to neutralize this concern by hosting the in-band virtualization software on multiprocessor PC platforms and by pro-

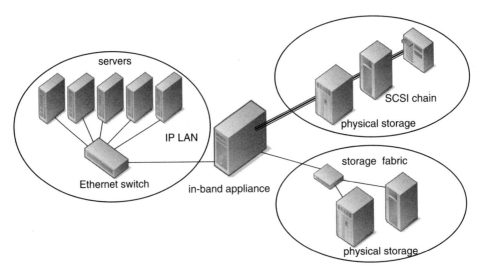

Figure 9.2 In-band virtualization may be implemented for Ethernet-attached servers with storage pooling of a mix of SCSI, Fibre Channel, SATA, SAS, or other storage drives.

viding large amounts of cache memory as compensation for read-intensive applications such as web hosting. In the two-tiered fabric scenario for Fibre Channel in-band virtualization, there is also the issue of transport latency, since data must pass through two separate fabrics to be served up to the hosts. Certainly for storage applications that only require moderate performance, congestion in the appliance may not occur or at least not be noticeable in terms of application response time. Higher performance applications, though, require that the appliance platform, processor speed, and cache memory be sized to the requisite bandwidth.

One significant advantage of in-band storage virtualization is its ability to enforce physical separation between servers and storage. Because the appliance is the intermediary between initiators and targets, it prevents servers from independently and inadvertently discovering and attaching to SAN-based storage assets, as might occur in a conventional SAN.

9.3 Out-of-Band Virtualization Appliances

Out-of-band virtualization appliances use separate paths for control information and data and thus place the appliance outside the primary path between servers and storage. As shown in Figure 9.3, an out-of-band appliance may attach to an existing Fibre Channel SAN as a peer on the storage network. The control path in this example is between the appliance and each SAN-attached server, switched directly through the fabric. Unlike in-band solutions, however, storage data does not pass through the appliance, but traverses the fabric directly between storage and servers. As out-of-band appliance vendors are quick to point out, this configuration eliminates the potential bottleneck issue, since only relatively small amounts of metadata are exchanged by the appliance and the servers. The out-of-band virtualization performance is thus largely determined by the performance of the SAN switch itself and the end devices.

Out-of-band virtualization appliances may also require host-resident drivers to maintain the virtualization mapping generated by the appliance and to pass exceptions to the appliance for processing. A 256 KB write operation to a striped virtual volume, for example, may need to be broken into four separate 64 KB write operations directed to four different storage targets. As with any storage application requiring software shims on servers, this places an additional burden on the vendor in terms of currency of operating system levels and on the customer to install and administer

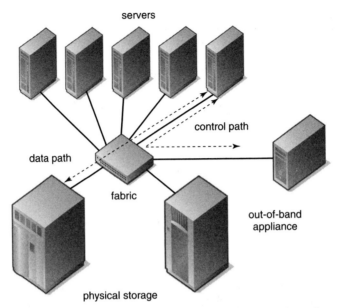

Figure 9.3 Out-of-band virtualization appliances attach to the storage network but do not intervene in the data path between servers and storage.

extra bits of code per server. Because the host-resident software is required for the server to access virtualized storage across the network, it cannot be installed on a network-attached storage device but should be loadable from direct-attached or IDE disk.

A significant advantage of out-of-band virtualization appliances is that they require no significant changes to the SAN infrastructure, relying instead on the SAN's ability to partition and isolate selected groups of devices. An out-of-band appliance simply attaches to the SAN, discovers the storage assets at its disposal, configures storage pools and corresponding LUNs under management control, and distributes block address mapping metadata to the client servers. This provides a relatively smooth migration path from conventional storage and virtualized storage on the SAN.

9.4 High Availability for Virtualization Appliances

Whether deployed as a dedicated hardware platform or installed on a PC, a single instance of the virtualization appliance cannot meet high availability requirements. Appliance vendors have therefore implemented various failover or distributed appliance solutions that enable the tasks of one appliance to be assumed by another. An active/passive configuration provides failover in the event that a primary appliance or path is down, but does not leverage the investment made for the two units. An active/active configuration is preferable, since it utilizes both appliance platforms and can provide load balancing in addition to failover.

As shown in Figure 9.4, a fully redundant in-band solution duplicates all connections, switches, and appliances. The servers in this case are provisioned with redundant HBAs, and thus are safeguarded in the event of an adapter card failure. The server fabric is built with two switches, each of

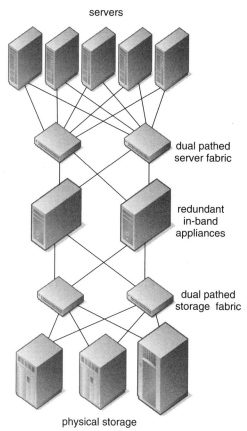

Figure 9.4 Providing high availability for in-band virtualization requires deployment of redundant fabric switches, appliances, and paths.

which has its own links to each server and to the virtualization appliances. Likewise, the storage fabric provides dual pathing between the storage arrays and redundant switches. Both the storage fabric and server fabric are dual-linked to each of the appliances. The in-band appliances in this example share metadata mapping information and exchange a status heartbeat either via the SAN or a dedicated Ethernet connection between the two. The failure of either appliance or any link to servers or storage will result in a failover to the appropriate alternate path or appliance. This high availability solution is scalable to additional appliances, but because the appliances must stand between servers and storage, adding additional appliances requires complete duplication of all paths.

A high availability configuration for out-of-band virtualization appliances is slightly less complicated, since the out-of-band device can simply attach to a dual-pathed SAN. As shown by Figure 9.5, the redundant HBAs, links, and switches typical of high availability SAN designs provide alternate routes between servers and storage should an HBA, link, or switch fail. In this example, the out-of-band appliances are attached to each redundant switch as additional SAN nodes. In an active/active configuration, both ap-

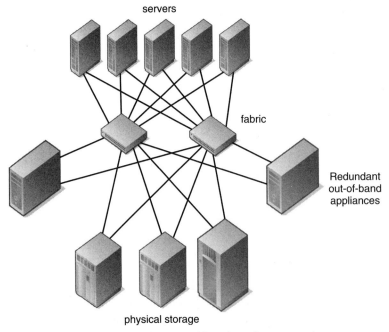

Figure 9.5 High availability for out-of-band appliances can be implemented with redundant units and links to a dual-pathed SAN.

pliances would share the task of metadata maintenance and monitor their mutual status via a Fibre Channel or Ethernet heartbeat connection.

Both the in-band and out-of-band high availability configurations could be supplemented with additional high availability SAN options such as server clustering, as well as virtualization services such as data replication and snapshots. Each increment in high availability, however, builds more complexity into the total installation and requires deliberate design and configuration. Providing everyone has done his or her job properly, a high availability solution should not require constant ongoing maintenance. Getting the entire configuration installed and stable in the first place is always the bulk of the work.

9.5 Appliances for Mass Consumption

Combined with iSCSI technology, the storage virtualization appliance architecture creates new opportunities to extend the benefits of shared and virtualized storage to a much broader market of departmental and small business applications. The development of low-cost virtualization appliances reflects the convergence of new storage networking technologies and the mass distribution of sophisticated functionality that was previously only available on enterprise-class SAN systems.

iSCSI offers an economical means to perform block SCSI I/O over affordable Ethernet infrastructures. Virtualization vendors aiming at the low end but very populous small and medium business market are combining iSCSI host connectivity with virtualization of legacy SCSI-attached disk arrays. This strategy enables customers to redeploy their existing SCSI assets and move from direct-attached storage to shared storage via a virtualization appliance.

As shown on the left in Figure 9.6, small IT shops typically manage storage assets through direct-attached SCSI connections. As with large enterprises, a DAS strategy is not easily scaled to larger configurations and perpetuates per-server management, over- and underutilization of storage and inefficient data backup operations. The combination of iSCSI host access over Ethernet and storage pooling of legacy SCSI disks, however, instantly delivers the core value of shared storage while incurring minimal investment in new equipment. Appliances in this class typically list at $15,000 or less, putting virtualization of storage within reach of a broad market well below the entry level established by Fibre Channel pricing.

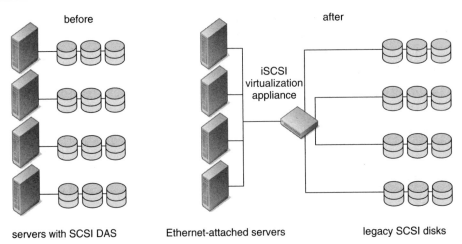

Figure 9.6 Low-cost storage virtualization is available through appliances that provide iSCSI host access and basic storage pooling capability.

As the adage goes, you get what you pay for. Low-cost virtualization appliances are not enterprise-class in scalability, performance, availability, or auxiliary service support. For departmental and small business application needs, though, they are suitable for moderate performance and represent a major step up compared to management of dispersed direct-attached storage arrays. Although vendors of larger, higher margin SAN solutions are not cheering the arrival of such low-cost appliances, such products will accelerate the proliferation of shared storage solutions and pave a migration path from smaller to larger solutions over time.

9.6 Chapter Summary

Black Box Virtualization

- A virtualization appliance is an intelligent processing platform that attaches to storage or a storage network.

- A virtualization appliance may be implemented on optimized hardware or as software that runs on a standard Wintel processor.

- Virtualization appliances can accommodate a variety of heterogeneous operating systems, host platforms, and storage targets from different vendors.

- Appliances may support Fibre Channel, iSCSI, or proprietary protocols for host access and Fibre Channel, iSCSI, SCSI, SATA, or SAS for storage.

In-Band Virtualization Appliances

- In-band virtualization appliances combine control information and data transport over the same path.

- The in-band virtualization device resides directly between servers and storage.

- An in-band virtualization appliance using Fibre Channel may require two separate fabrics for server and storage connectivity.

- An in-band appliance is a target to the client servers and an initiator to the back-end storage devices.

- Potential performance bottlenecks for in-band virtualization may be overcome with processing speed and cache memory.

Out-of-Band Virtualization Appliances

- Out-of-band virtualization separates control information paths from data paths.

- An out-of-band appliance attaches to a storage network as a peer node.

- In an out-of-band virtualization solution, servers access data directly through the SAN.

- Out-of-band virtualization may require host-resident software or hardware to maintain virtualization block address mapping.

- Out-of-band virtualization typically requires no change to the SAN infrastructure design.

High Availability for Virtualization Appliances

- A single virtualization appliance represents a potential single point of failure.

- High availability for virtualization appliances requires dual pathing through the SAN and redundant appliances for failover.

- In an active/active configuration, redundant appliances may perform load balancing as well as failover capability.

■ Redundant appliances exchange status via an Ethernet or Fibre Channel heartbeat protocol.

Appliances for Mass Consumption

■ The combination of iSCSI and virtualization technology is enabling low-cost but sophisticated shared storage solutions.

■ Economical iSCSI virtualization appliances may repurpose legacy direct-attached storage to provide virtualized shared storage.

■ Lowcost iSCSI virtualization appliances provide a migration path from small to large shared storage networking.

10 Virtualization Services

PRESENTING DISPARATE STORAGE assets as a common resource that can be efficiently allocated on demand is the foundation of storage virtualization. Once physical assets have been virtualized, additional value-added services can be enabled to further reduce administrative overhead. This chapter reviews the storage services that are facilitated by virtualization, including heterogeneous mirroring, data replication, snapshots, and hierarchical storage management through virtualized classes of storage and virtualized backup operations.

10.1 Enabling Advanced Storage Services

Storage virtualization is a technical means to what are essentially business ends. Business in this sense applies to both commercial and noncommercial (government, institutional, or nonprofit) entities. Reducing the cost of data storage administration, maximizing utilization of storage assets, dynamically aligning data storage capacity to changing application requirements, ensuring high availability access to data, and safeguarding an organization's information are common requirements for every institution and enterprise.

On its own, masking the complexity of physical storage systems provides value by enabling administrators to manage more storage capacity more efficiently. Virtualizing storage, however, does not ensure that data will be protected or available in the event of failures or disruptions. Auxiliary services are therefore required to provide data protection and high availability for the virtualized storage assets.

Services such as mirroring, data replication, and hierarchical storage management are not dependent on storage virtualization and can be implemented in homogeneous, single-vendor, nonvirtualized environments.

Whether by choice or the happenstance of mergers and acquisitions, most companies have at least some mix of heterogeneous storage. Without storage virtualization, each vendor storage system would require its own proprietary solution to support high availability and data protection, resulting in additional administration, licensing costs, and expense in duplicating vendor-specific storage arrays. Virtualizing storage systems filters out these proprietary requirements and provides the enabling foundation for implementing advanced storage services through a single cross-vendor application.

The tradeoff for uniformity and simplicity in this case is sacrifice of vendor-specific value-added capabilities. Disk-to-disk data replication, for example, is supported in some proprietary form by every provider of storage systems. These applications are fine-tuned to the specific architectures of each vendor and so offer performance and reliability enhancements that only operate in homogeneous environments. Virtualizing these systems effectively disables many value-added benefits. Due diligence is therefore required to weigh the advantages and disadvantages of virtualizing heterogeneous storage systems to enable advanced vendor-neutral services. In some cases, the loss of value-added features may be an unacceptable tradeoff.

Vendors that offer both system-level virtualization of their own arrays and proprietary advanced services such as data replication provide both simplification of storage administration and value-added features, although still in a single-vendor context. Customers that are comfortable with homogeneous storage can at least enjoy the benefits of multi-array virtualization while retaining proprietary services, but will have fewer options if a third-party array suddenly appears in their data center.

10.2 Pooling Heterogeneous Storage Assets

In a conventional storage network, storage arrays are configured to support specific LUNs that are assigned to individual servers. In some storage products, the size of these assigned LUNs may be modified as capacity requirements increase, but typically only within a single storage unit. Without some form of virtualization, it is not possible to borrow additional disk banks from a neighboring SAN-attached array.

As shown in Figure 10.1, the preconfigured LUNs of each physical storage array are announced to the storage network and under administrative control bound to the appropriate servers. Server 1 in this example has at its disposal LUN 8 from Array A (Vendor X) and LUN 55 from Array C (Vendor Z). Unfortunately for Server 1, the storage blocks in LUN 55 are fully utilized. Server 3 is assigned LUN 43 from Array B (Vendor Y), as well as LUN 22. In this case, the data blocks supported by LUN 22 are being used by an application that will never utilize more than a third of the blocks allocated for it. This was not known to the administrator when the LUN was originally defined. The common result is that the often considerable investment in the SAN and SAN-attached storage is not fully maximized, which in turn may require additional investments in storage units despite the availability of unused capacity on other arrays.

As is evident from Figure 10.1, SANs provide shared access to storage devices but do not automatically enable consolidation of storage systems or efficient utilization of storage capacity across systems. Consolidation

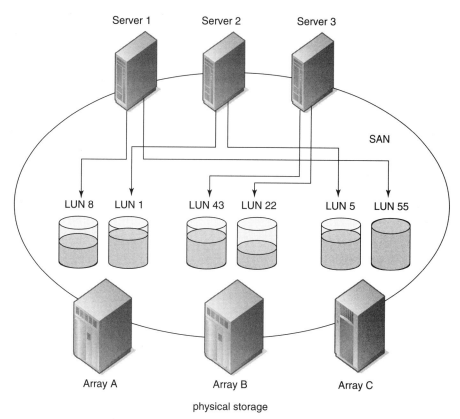

Figure 10.1 Storage allocation in a conventional, nonvirtualized SAN is restricted to a direct assignment of physical assets to individual servers. Over- and under capacity utilization can only be addressed per physical storage array.

requires a virtualization layer above the individual storage arrays, generated somewhere within the SAN (host, array, fabric, or appliance).

As shown in Figure 10.2, a virtualized storage pool is typically depicted as an extended storage container that represents the total storage capacity of all arrays under virtualization control. Virtualized LUNs that are presented to servers may therefore draw upon disk banks that reside on different physical storage units and can be dynamically resized to match changing application requirements.

In terms of simplifying storage administration, the initial configuration of the storage pool from physical arrays still requires careful and deliberate manual administration, although graphical interfaces provided by virtualization vendors are helping to streamline installation. Day-to-day administration, however, benefits from the aggregation of multiple per-array management tasks into management of a single large, virtualized storage

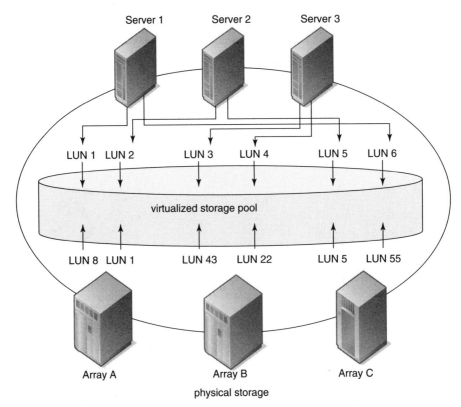

Figure 10.2 In a virtualized storage pool, virtual assets may be dynamically resized and allocated to servers by drawing on the total storage capacity of the SAN.

entity. The administrator in effect manages the virtualization engine, which in turn is responsible for managing discrete vendor-specific storage arrays under its control.

Pooling of heterogeneous storage assets may also include pooling of dissimilar storage products such as high end, highly available RAID systems and low-cost JBODs. Because not all storage is created equal, the democratization of sophisticated systems and fairly simple disk systems in the same storage pool does not elevate the capabilities of low-end systems or establish a norm somewhere between high-end and low-end. So although JBOD storage may be assigned as a data replication target for a high-end RAID array, that would not be a best practices recommendation. If the RAID array fails or is taken offline, the JBOD would be an unsuitable choice for assuming production responsibilities. On the other hand, coexistence in the same storage pool simplifies assignment of class of storage to different applications. The capacity of one or more JBODs in a pool may be assigned to noncritical applications, and the administrator has the flexibility of borrowing capacity from higher end systems if the collective JBOD capacity is exceeded.

Allocating resources from a heterogeneous pool also requires attention to high availability requirements for specific applications. Some storage arrays, for example, support alternate pathing at the storage port level. If a particular path fails, the array can recognize and respond to the outage and maintain data transactions on the remaining path. To build high availability into the SAN infrastructure that can then be leveraged by a storage virtualization entity requires that the capacity of pooled arrays assigned to a specific application have similar functionality, even if the arrays are from different vendors. This ensures that quality of service can be maintained, despite the generic reduction of the storage abstraction layer.

In addition, the performance requirements of specific applications should be taken into consideration. One of the key drivers for storage virtualization is the ability to leverage unused capacity in storage systems via storage pooling. A database application, for example, may only be using half of a storage system's total capacity, and it is attractive to think that the other half can be put into a storage pool and be dynamically assigned to other servers or applications. The database program, however, may be using 99% of the array's IO capability, in which case pooling the unused storage capacity and assigning it elsewhere would severely impact database performance.

10.3 Heterogeneous Mirroring

As discussed in section 5.1.2 of Chapter 5, Abstracting Physical Storage, storage virtualization enables mirroring or synchronized local data copying between dissimilar storage systems. Because the virtualization engine processes the SCSI I/O to physical storage and is represented as a single storage target to the server, virtualized mirroring can offer more flexible options than conventional disk-to-disk techniques.

In traditional single-vendor environments, mirroring is typically performed within a single array (one set of disk banks to another) or between adjacent arrays. Disk mirroring may be active/passive, in that the secondary mirror is only brought into service if the primary array fails, or active/active, in which case the secondary mirror can be accessed for read operations if the primary is busy. This both increases performance and enhances the value of the secondary mirror. In addition, some vendors provide mutual mirroring between disk arrays so that each array acts as a secondary mirror to its partner.

Heterogeneous mirroring under virtualization control allows mirroring operations to be configured from any physical storage assets and for any level of redundancy. As shown in Figure 10.3, a server may perform traditional read and write operations to a virtualized primary volume. The target entity within the virtualization engine processes each write operation and acts as an initiator to copy it to two separate mirrors. The virtual mirrors, as well as the virtualized primary volume, may be composed of storage blocks from any combination of back-end physical storage arrays. In this example, the secondary mirror could be used to convenience non-disruptive storage processes such as archiving disk data to tape or migration of data from one class of storage to another.

Like traditional disk-based mirroring, this virtualized solution may be transparent to the host system, providing there is no significant performance impact in executing copies to heterogeneous storage. Transparency assumes, though, that the virtualizing is conducted by the fabric or an appliance attached to the fabric. Host-based virtualization would consume CPU cycles to perform multiple mirroring, and array-based virtualization typically cannot cross vendor lines. Because mirroring requires the completion of writes on the secondary mirrors before the next I/O is accepted, performance is largely dependent on the aggregate capabilities of the physical storage systems and the processing power of the virtualization engine itself.

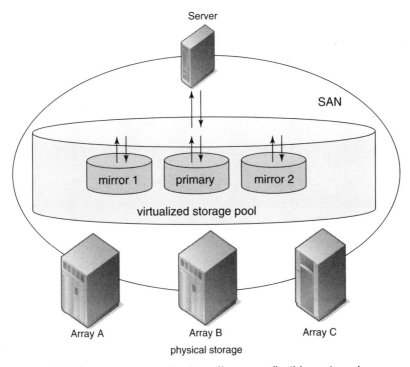

Figure 10.3 Heterogeneous mirroring offers more flexible options than conventional mirroring, including three-way mirroring within storage capacity carved from different storage systems.

10.4 Heterogeneous Data Replication

Data replication differs from mirroring in that data copying is performed between storage systems that are typically separated geographically by distance. Like local mirroring, synchronous data replication requires that each write complete status on the secondary array be confirmed before the next write operation is processed. Due to the latency contributed by speed of light propagation over distance (roughly 1 millisecond per 100 miles), synchronous data replication is limited to metropolitan distances of about 150 miles (300 miles or 3 milliseconds latency round trip). Asynchronous data replication provides local write complete status once the data is written to the primary array, but buffers the write data and sends it asynchronously to the secondary array. Asynchronous data replication is therefore relatively insensitive to latency over distance (to thousands of miles), but cannot ensure that every current transaction is captured. A loss of a wide area link, for example, may result in inconsistency in images between the primary and secondary arrays. The primary array would have already processed the most recent write operation, but the secondary would not.

Every major storage vendor provides its own proprietary versions of synchronous and asynchronous data replication. EMC's Symmetrix Remote Data Facility (SRDF) for Symmetrix systems and MirrorView for CLARi-iON arrays, IBM's Peer to Peer Remote Copy (PPRC) for Shark arrays, and HDS's TrueCopy for the HDS 9900 series arrays, for example, provide the same basic functionality in synchronous and asynchronous flavors, but each can only be run on its respective proprietary hardware platform. The ability to perform synchronous or asynchronous data replication between hetero-geneous storage systems is therefore an attractive option for customers with mixed storage environments or who are in transition from one vendor to another.

In conventional disk-to-disk data replication, the primary disk array hosts both initiator and target functions. To the servers issuing data reads and writes, the array is a target. To the secondary array receiving write op-erations, the primary array is an initiator. The array-based initiator must monitor the status of the replicated writes and handle exceptions if faults occur.

Heterogeneous data replication via virtualization moves the replication initiator function to the virtualization engine residing somewhere within the SAN. Because the volumes being written to may be virtualized from diverse physical storage systems, the "disk-to-disk" data replication theoretically may be from data blocks on the primary multiple systems to data blocks on the secondary multiple systems. In practice, however, the virtualized data replication is implemented from one storage system to another, and the value of virtualizing in this case simply to perform cross-vendor replication.

As shown in Figure 10.4, virtual volumes have been configured on a storage system from Vendor A at a primary production facility. The produc-tion servers read and write to those volumes under the direction of the local storage virtualization entity. Local write transactions to the Vendor A sys-tem are monitored by the virtualizer and copied to a peer virtualization de-vice at a remote site. The remote storage system in this case is provided by Vendor C, which without virtualization would have no means to replicate data from Vendor A's hardware.

Some virtualization vendors offer Ethernet interfaces on their virtualiza-tion appliances to facilitate remote block data replication using iSCSI over

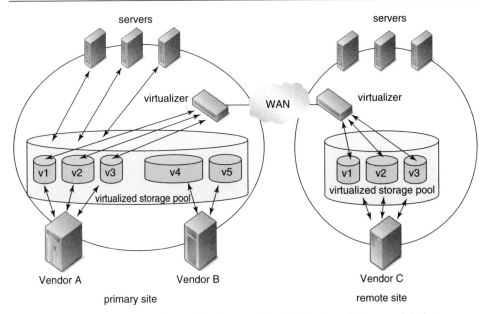

Figure 10.4 Heterogeneous data replication enables duplication of storage data between otherwise incompatible storage systems. Synchronous replication may be performed over metropolitan distances; asynchronous replication may be extended across thousands of miles.

an IP infrastructure. Others rely on optimized storage over IP gateways (IP SAN routers) attached to the SAN to provide the wide area transport. In either case, the classic goal of data replication to provide high availability data access for disaster recovery and other storage applications is met, as well as accommodation of otherwise incompatible storage systems.

10.5 Point-in-Time Data Snapshots

Traditionally, high availability data access has been supported through local mirroring and data replication at the storage system level, directors and dual pathing in the SAN infrastructure, and clustering software for servers. For storage, mirroring and data replication provide a safeguard against the failure of an array or main production facility. These techniques, however, do not guard against data corruption that may occur, for example, through a virus or other malevolent intrusion. If corrupt data is written to a primary array, it is simply duplicated on the secondary array, with or without the assistance of storage virtualization. Snapshot technology provides a means to

roll back a storage image to a known point in time, either to retrieve data
that has been changed inadvertently, or to recover to a point of valid data in
the event of corruption.

As shown in Figure 10.5, a virtual volume has been created from physical disk assets from Arrays A, B, and C. As the server continually updates
data on the virtual volume, point-in-time copies are performed on a periodic basis. In this example, snapshots are taken every four hours. The snapshots do not copy the entire virtual volume, but contain the original data
that was modified after the snapshot was taken. This makes it possible to
reconstruct a volume image to a given point in time. If, for example, the virtual volume supports a Microsoft Exchange application and a virus is dis-
covered at 4:00 P.M., the virtual volume can be restored to a previous
uninfected state, e.g., 12:00 P.M. or 8:00 A.M. With snapshots, some data

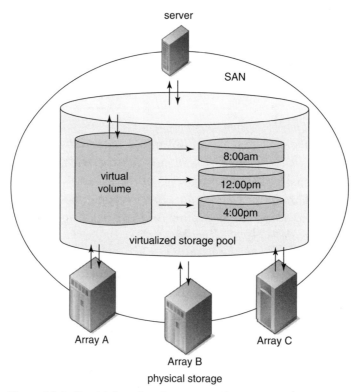

Figure 10.5 Combining virtual storage with snapshot capability
provides more granular control over data retrieval compared to
mirroring or data replication. Point in time images of storage data
can be reconstructed in the event of data corruption.

transactions will be lost, but unlike data corruption in a mirror or data replication scenario, it is possible to salvage the bulk of known good data and quickly resume operations.

Just as the virtual volume may be composed of data blocks from multiple storage arrays, the storage capacity required for the snapshots may be drawn from a variety of disk assets. The maximum number of potential snapshots is therefore quite large, depending on the aggregate capacity of the storage pool.

Virtualization products may provide snapshot utilities that span several weeks of point-in-time copies or a greater frequency of snapshots for applications that constantly modify data. A virtual volume that is used to service web hosting, for example, would not require frequent snapshots; a virtual volume supporting an online order entry application would. Snapshots are also useful for other purposes, such as application development and tape backup. Because snapshots do not disrupt ongoing data transactions, previous snapshots can be used to test new applications against nearly current data and to perform nonintrusive tape backup at periodic intervals.

10.6 Hierarchical Storage Management

Hierarchical storage management (also referred to as data lifecycle management or information lifecycle management) focuses on the transition of data from its active application state to eventual archiving on tape or optical media. Current data transactions may require immediate accessibility and protection via RAID, mirroring, data replication, or snapshots. As data ages, it may still require accessibility (e.g., retrieving an email sent four months ago), but some delay in access may be acceptable. As data enters its golden years, however, it may be put out to pasture for long-term storage on tape or optical media. Today's government regulatory requirements generally forbid data euthanasia, and for legal purposes companies must be prepared to recall records and files accumulated over many years. Streamlining the management of data through its lifecycle and migrating it to the appropriate classes of storage for retrieval, therefore, has significant value for enterprises that must cope with the steady onslaught of new data while managing massive amounts of previously generated data.

In addition, data that no longer has currency for active applications may have substantial value for secondary applications. Records generated by online order entry, for example, not only detail past transactions but also may contain a wealth of data for demographic and market trending analysis. In this case, storage for data mining may be a secondary phase in data lifecycle as it passes from an active application state to further processing to extract its value.

Storage virtualization is an enabling foundation for hierarchical storage and data lifecycle management. Because virtualization inserts intelligent abstraction between servers and physical storage, it is positioned to automate the migration of real storage data from one virtualized resource to another over time. As shown in Figure 10.6, a storage network may provide connectivity for diverse storage assets, ranging from high availability RAID systems (HA RAID A and B) to generic RAID arrays (RAID C), JBODs (JBOD D and E), tape, and optical storage subsystems. The virtualized volumes supporting active application data (V1 and V2) are created from block ranges on the high availability RAID systems and may be configured via virtualization for mirroring (mV1), data replication (rV2), or snapshots (sV1) on some combination of high availability RAID or generic, lower cost RAID.

As the portions of the data originally committed to V1 and V2 age and lose their immediate value for active application use, they may be migrated to secondary online virtual volumes (V3) drawn from block ranges on JBODs. In this example, the JBOD-based virtual volume is mirrored (mV3) to retain data availability through the aging process. Although the virtual volumes carved from JBOD assets do not provide the performance and robustness of RAID systems, they provide an economical means to maintain online access to less frequently used data before it is passed to an archive. Finally, as online accessibility is no longer required, the data may be migrated via a temporary volume (V5) for commitment to tape, and eventually to optical media.

Like other virtualization services, hierarchical storage management requires additional intelligence to execute the appropriate movement of data from one asset to another. That intelligence may be in the form of additional utilities provided by a virtualization application or a third-party management application that leverages virtualized resources to facilitate data migration behind the scenes. This further highlights the value of standardization initiatives such as FAIS and SMI-S in defining common APIs for communication between the virtual storage world and storage management platforms.

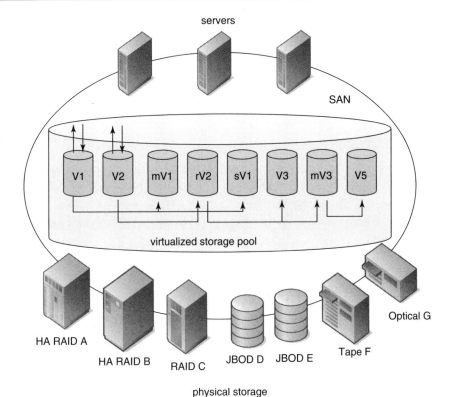

Figure 10.6 Storage virtualization facilitates the migration of data from one class of storage to another as data passes from its immediate availability to eventual archiving on long-term storage such as tape or optical media.

Hierarchical storage management ultimately depends on tiered storage capabilities of different physical devices that reflect different performance and cost attributes. Classes of storage for SAN-attached block devices have not been canonized by industry standards but can be assembled in the following hierarchy:

Class 1: High-availability, high-performance RAID systems

Class 2: Moderate performance RAID systems

Class 3: Solid-state memory storage systems

Class 4: Fibre Channel JBODs

Class 5: Custom disk-to-disk-to-tape systems

Class 6: High-performance tape libraries

Class 7: Moderate-performance tape subsystems and devices

Class 8: Optical jukeboxes

This classification is not based on a single criterion such as performance, but on a combination of performance, reliability, and cost considerations. Solid-state memory storage (a.k.a. ramdisks), for example, provide high performance but at a high cost and with less reliability than Fibre Channel RAID systems. Consequently, some solid-state storage products use Fibre Channel disks on the back end to copy data in the event of a power outage. Likewise, high-performance tape libraries are expensive, but their performance is high only in relation to other tape subsystems. Disk will always be faster for data retrieval than tape. All of these physical storage systems transport block data with standard SCSI protocols, thus all are the potential participants in a virtualized storage solution. Automated data aging and migration between classes of storage therefore provides flexibility in solution design, depending on the requirements of specific customer applications.

10.7 Chapter Summary

Enabling Advanced Storage Services
- Virtualizing storage systems does not ensure data protection or availability.

- Mirroring, data replication, and other services are not dependent on virtualization, but are easier to implement in heterogeneous environment.

- Storage virtualization filters out proprietary requirements of storage systems and establishes a common interface across vendor boundaries.

- To preserve vendor value-added features, a storage vendor may supply virtualization for homogeneous storage.

Pooling Heterogeneous Storage Assets
- Storage pooling allows disk resources from multiple systems to be configured as a single virtual volume.

- SANs provide connectivity for storage sharing but have no inherent storage consolidation capability.

- Installation of a storage pool requires deliberate and careful manual administration.

- Ongoing administration of a storage pool is simplified because the virtualization engine manages the multiple physical storage systems under its control.

- Storage pooling allows for aggregation of multi-vendor storage devices.

Heterogeneous Mirroring

- Mirroring provides synchronized local data copying between two arrays.

- Virtualization enables mirroring between otherwise incompatible storage devices.

- Active/passive mirroring assumes that the secondary mirror is only accessed in the event of failure of the primary array.

- Active/active mirroring allows either primary and secondary arrays to be accessed for data reads.

- Virtualization facilitates the creation of multiple mirrors.

- Transparent heterogeneous mirroring may be performed by array-based, fabric-based, or appliance-based virtualization entities.

Heterogeneous Data Replication

- Synchronous data replication requires that each write operation is completed on a secondary array before another write I/O can be processed.

- Asynchronous data replication acknowledges write completion locally while caching the write operation for transport to the secondary array.

- Asynchronous data replication results in inconsistency in data images between primary and secondary storage arrays.

- Synchronous data replication is limited to metropolitan distances (~150 miles).

- Asynchronous data replication may be extended to thousands of miles.

- All storage providers offer synchronous and asynchronous data replication applications for their products.

- Storage virtualization enables data replication to be performed between incompatible storage systems.

- Some virtualization products include interfaces for IP transport of replication traffic over distance.

Point-in-Time Data Snapshots

- Mirroring and data replication cannot guard against data corruption.

- Snapshots provide point-in-time copies of a storage volume.

- A snapshot contains the delta changes in data blocks since the last snapshot was taken.

- A storage volume can be restored to a known good state using snapshot information.

- Recovery to a particular point-in-time snapshot may result in the loss of some transactions.

- Frequency of snapshots should be determined by the rate of data change for a particular application.

Hierarchical Storage Management

- Hierarchical storage management migrates block data between classes of storage based on accessibility requirements of data over time.

- Data lifecycle management is useful for auxiliary applications such as data mining.

- Storage virtualization facilitates hierarchical storage management by inserting network intelligence between classes of storage.

- Classes of storage are defined by performance, reliability, and cost factors and can be paired with the current requirements of specific application data.

11 Virtualized SAN File Systems

VIRTUALIZATION OF BLOCK DATA storage systems facilitates services such as storage consolidation and efficient capacity utilization, but does not automatically enable sharing of data at the file level. This chapter provides an overview of file system virtualization, which further abstracts the physical from logical view of data and enables a more granular sharing of data.

11.1 Conventional File Systems

Files systems reside on logical volumes that in turn are constructed of real or virtualized LUNs drawn from physical disks. An individual file appears as a contiguous stream of bytes with unique attributes such as a file name, ownership, time of creation/modification, read/write permissions, and so on as contained in the file metadata. The contiguous bytes of data that compose a file are rarely contiguous on disk, however, but may be discrete blocks of data bytes dispersed accidentally (e.g., fragmentation) or purposefully (e.g., block striping) on one or more disks.

File metadata is for the most part segregated from the file content via a master file table (Windows) or super block (Unix). In conventional file systems, the file metadata is stored at a specific location on a logical volume and is visible only to the server that is bound to that volume or LUN. The file metadata is persistent, however, and if one server is replaced by another, the new server running the same OS will see the same file system as the original. Because such sequential access does not equal file sharing, sharing individual files requires multiple servers to have concurrent visibility to a common file system structure.

As illustrated in Figure 11.1, a SAN enables sharing of a large storage resource such as a RAID system between multiple servers. The capacity of the

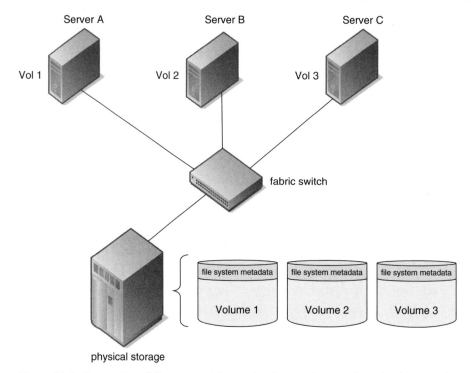

Figure 11.1 Conventional file system information is stored per assigned volume and is accessible to only one server. Sharing of individual files between multiple servers requires common access to file metadata via a distributed file system.

storage system is divided into LUNs from a storage hardware perspective and logical volumes from a server software perspective. Each server is assigned one or more logical volumes for its use, on which it stores the operating system, auxiliary files, application code, and user-generated data, all in the logical structure of a file system dedicated to that server. The aggregate file metadata contained in the master file table or super block is simply another form of data to be stored as data blocks on disk. In this case, because the data is special and absolutely essential for system operation, it may be written to multiple specific locations on one or more logical volumes.

Storage virtualization alters this picture in that the logical volumes and associated LUNs may live on multiple and sometimes very different physical storage arrays. Nonetheless, the exclusive ownership by a server of its designated volumes is unchanged, despite the abstraction of physical storage assets. If an unauthorized server gains simultaneous access to another server's logical volume, mayhem in the form of continual disk checking (e.g., chkdsk in Windows) will occur on both servers as each attempts to reconcile the sudden and for each unexplainable appearance of inconsistencies in the file system structure. Storage virtualization is the innocent bystander in this case, since it can do nothing to protect data at the file level, which sits on top of virtualized block storage. Typically, HBAs, switches, or storage arrays provide basic LUN mapping or masking as a means to restrict server access.

11.2 Distributed File Systems

File sharing can be accomplished by using standard network file access protocols such as network file system (NFS) or the common Internet file system (CIFS). Use of NFS and CIFS enables shared file access between clients on different operating system platforms, but assumes the existence of a network-attached file server. The file server has exclusive access to the file metadata and serves as a single point of arbitration for the access requests made by the client systems.

Network-attached storage (NAS) provides shared file access, but not direct delivery of block SCSI data between storage targets and initiators. In addition, a NFS or CIFS client must still have its own storage to at least support booting of the operating system and loading the requisite NFS or CIFS device drivers—i.e., it must already have a loaded file system before it mounts the NAS storage as additional volumes.

Distributed or global file systems are a specialized file system layer shared in common by multiple servers concurrently. Every server has the same view of the file system and therefore access to subdirectories and individual files. This universal access has an inherent vulnerability to file corruption, since without a file-locking mechanism, any server could change any portion of a file (or delete it) at will, regardless of how many other servers were working on the same file. A distributed file system must therefore support a robust and fairly sophisticated file-locking routine, with time-stamps to monitor file changes and communication between servers to alert their peers when a file is under concurrent access or processing.

A distributed file system scheme on its own is not yet file system virtualization and does not require underlying virtualization of storage assets. As in the example cited for Figure 11.1, Servers A, B, and C could have concurrent access to Volumes 1, 2, and 3, with a direct mapping between those volumes and the physical disk array supporting them. The file system metadata still resides on each volume, but now under the collective access and control of the cooperating servers (a.k.a. cluster file system).

11.3 Virtualizing File Systems

Virtualization of storage systems is predicated on an abstraction layer between the logical presentation of storage volumes to servers and the physical data blocks supporting them. The bridge between virtual assets and real ones is provided by storage metadata, which maps virtual locations to physical locations. File system virtualization likewise requires an abstraction layer, which is implemented on top of the storage virtualization layer. The bridge between the virtual file system and the actual structure of files is provided by file metadata, which masks the actual distribution and paths to directories and files from the presentation of the virtual file system to servers.

In a virtualized file system, the universal accessibility of the file system to multiple heterogeneous servers is based on a global name space that allows a file system hierarchy to be built on top of potentially diverse storage volumes. This global name space supplements a server's local name space or file system. A server, for example, may still have exclusive ownership of its C: drive, from which it loads an operating system and requisite device drivers. In reality, that C: drive volume may reside somewhere on the SAN, generated from pooled storage systems, but assigned to the server's sole use. A global name space appears, via file system virtualization, as another volume—e.g., M: drive. In reality, the M: drive may be composed of a structure that spans multiple virtualized volumes and is shared by multiple servers. Accommodation of this unique extension of a global file system may be provided by the operating system itself. Windows, for example, supports an installable file system (IFS) and Unix provides a virtual file system (VFS) connector for attaching third-party virtualization client software.

Because there is no direct correlation between the virtualized file system and a particular storage volume, file system metadata must be segregated to its own dedicated volume and accessible to the client servers under centralized control. This function is provided by one or more metadata servers connected to the SAN. As client servers access directories or files within the virtualized file system, their requests are redirected to the metadata servers. The metadata servers maintain the mapping to the actual location of specific files and are positioned to provide file locking and time stamp services.

Having been provided the path to a file's contents, the servers can access the data via block transport directly over the SAN.

As shown in Figure 11.2, file system metadata servers attach as peers to the SAN and so are accessible to all client servers over a high-performance infrastructure. This is a classic out-of-band configuration in that the metadata servers only pass control information to the servers, while the data path is provided through the fabric to virtual volumes in a storage pool. In this example, the file system metadata resides on its own dedicated virtual volume, v1. The remaining virtual volumes are the containers for the files represented by the virtual file system.

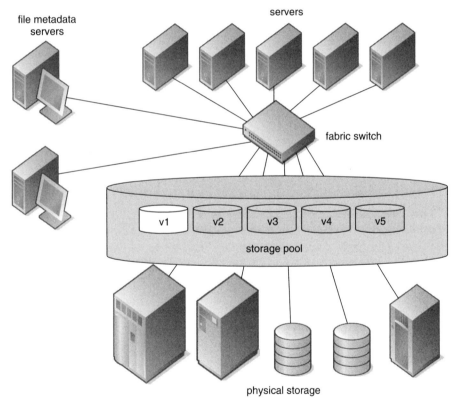

Figure 11.2 In a virtualized file system, file metadata servers provide mapping information for the location of discrete files within the virtualized file system hierarchy. Servers can then retrieve the data blocks associated with a file directly across the storage network.

Analogous to NFS and CIFS, the client software running on each server that provides redirection to the metadata servers enables a common file access method for different operating systems. IBM's SAN File System, for example, supports file system virtualization for Linux, Solaris, AIX, and Windows 2000 clients. Common access to a virtual file system, however, does not imply interoperability between heterogeneous applications. A Linux server and Windows server may have common access to a particular file, but the applications running on those servers may not be able to recognize or process the file contents.

For homogeneous application environments, a global, virtualized file system enables massive parallel processing of shared file data. Hundreds of Linux servers in a scientific application, for example, can operate on the same data concurrently to expedite processing. The main benefit of file system virtualization, though, is to streamline file system management and ongoing administration. Even if there is no file sharing, the aggregation of files into one virtualized file system provides a single point of management and helps reduce duplication of applications and files, facilitates licensing and application updates, and enables more efficient utilization of the underlying storage capacity.

High availability for virtualized file systems is provided by failover between file system metadata servers and reinforced by high-availability measures that have been implemented within the storage pool (e.g., mirroring or data replication between virtual volumes). Certainly, the volume containing the file system metadata should be protected via mirroring and RAID 5 to ensure the highest level of availability.

Building file system virtualization on top of storage virtualization provides a very scalable solution over time. The size of the metadata volume as well as user volumes can be dynamically increased to accommodate data growth, and multiple metadata servers can be provisioned to handle increasing workloads of additional servers. In addition, embedded virtualization services such as data lifecycle management can be used to migrate portions of the virtualized file system to different classes of storage depending on the access requirements of files as they age.

11.4 Chapter Summary

Conventional File Systems
- File systems reside on logical volumes drawn from actual or virtualized LUNs.

- File metadata specifies specific file attributes such as ownership, time stamps, and read/write permissions.

- A file's data contents may be distributed over multiple storage blocks on one or more disks.

- File metadata may be segregated from file content via a master file table or super block.

- A conventional file system is accessible only to an individual server.

Distributed File Systems

- Network file protocols such as NFS and CIFS provide shared file access but not direct delivery of block SCSI data composing a file.

- Distributed file systems provide common access to a file system hierarchy by multiple servers.

- Discrete file sharing requires a shared file locking mechanism to prevent overwriting of contents.

- A distributed file system does not mandate storage virtualization and can be implemented on physical storage devices.

Virtualizing File Systems

- File system virtualization imposes an abstraction layer between the presentation of the file system and its actual deployment on storage volumes.

- A virtualized file system provides a single global name space accessible to multiple servers.

- A virtualized file system appears as an additional storage drive.

- Windows installable file system (IFS) and Unix virtual file system (VFS) provide connectivity to a virtual file system.

- File system metadata resides on a dedicated virtual volume.

- File system metadata servers maintain mapping information on file attributes and location.

- Virtualized file systems may be accessible to heterogeneous client servers.

■ Common access to a virtual file system does not ensure interoperability at the application layer.

■ The main benefit of file system virtualization is simplified management.

■ High availability for virtualized file systems is provided by redundant metadata servers and high availability in the storage pool.

■ Virtualized file systems are scalable through the addition of metadata servers and dynamic expansion of virtual volumes in a storage pool.

12 Virtual Tape

VIRTUALIZATION TECHNOLOGY THAT FIRST emerged for disk systems is now expanding its reach to tape and other long-term removable storage media. Tape virtualization solutions promise to overcome the historical performance issues associated with tape backup and recovery and provide innovative alternatives for near-line storage. This chapter provides an overview of tape backup processes and the application of virtualization concepts to long-term data protection.

12.1 Conventional Tape Backup

With the ever-declining costs of disk media, many industry analysts have been predicting the demise of tape libraries, reels, and cartridges and their replacement by more readily accessible spinning disk media. These predictions have been made for years, yet tape backup is still a permanent fixture in enterprise data centers. In the meantime, tape technology has evolved to higher levels of performance and economy and the per-megabyte cost of tape storage is still a fraction of comparable disk media. Even as new serial ATA disk prices apply more competitive pressure to tape, tape is not disappearing but simply shifting to the right to accommodate a new player in the backup chain. As discussed below, disk-to-disk to tape (D2D2T) solutions have not fundamentally altered the role of tape for long-term data protection.

Traditional LAN-based tape backup has proven unsuitable for large enterprises, both due to the additional traffic load it imposes on the LAN and performance limitations when large numbers of servers execute backups. As shown in Figure 12.1, conventional storage backup presents a number of challenges, particularly for direct-attached storage. LAN-based backup solutions typically cannot accommodate the requirements of large server

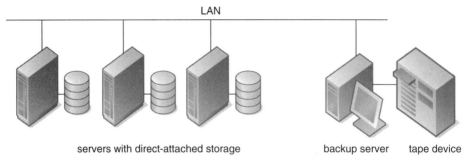

Figure 12.1 Traditional LAN-based tape backup incurs heavy traffic loads on the local area network and may not accommodate concurrent backup of multiple servers.

populations, which in turn results in the installation of additional backup servers and tape devices and accompanying higher administrative costs. Centralizing backup operations has been one of the main drivers of SAN technology, since it removes backup traffic from the LAN and leverages SAN bandwidth to accommodate concurrent backup streams.

In the example shown in Figure 12.1, the backup may be accomplished using block or file transport. If a file-level backup is performed, the backup server must maintain a separate catalog of file entries and file metadata for data retrieval. In the case of block-level backup, the entire disk volume or block delta changes may be sent to tape.

Implementing servers, storage, and tape on a SAN offers both performance advantages for tape backup as well as streamlined administration. As depicted in Figure 12.2, the SAN provides a high-performance block data transport for efficiently moving data to a SAN-attached tape system. Server-based backup as performed by Server B, however, still requires the server to copy data from the storage array and write it back to the tape device across the SAN. This consumes CPU cycles and results in inefficient use of both server and SAN fabric resources. The SAN path now established between storage arrays and tape systems via the fabric switch enables use of a third-party agent to act on behalf of the server. SCSI third party copy (TPC) may be run on a tape system, a fabric switch, or a dedicated device on the SAN. This server-free backup solution removes the server from the backup data path and provides a more direct route between disk and tape resources.

Although SAN-attached tape devices and libraries use standard SCSI protocols for block data movement, they vary widely in capabilities, capacities, and tape formats. Consequently, tape backup applications may offer

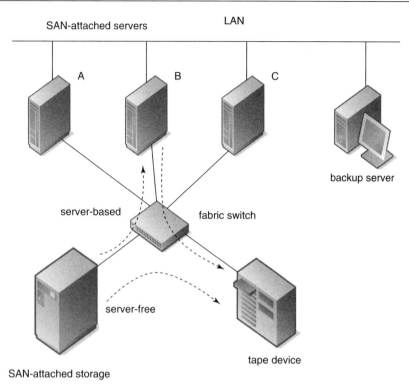

Figure 12.2 SAN-based backup removes backup traffic from the LAN and facilitates advanced backup services such as server-free backup. Server-free backup takes the server out of the backup data path via a third-party copy agent.

differing levels of support for vendor-specific tape libraries. In addition, customers may have a mix of open systems and proprietary platforms such as IBM OS/390 mainframes or IBM AS/400 midrange systems, each with its own unique backup requirements. Even with the efficiencies provided by SANs for backup operations, further consolidation of backup operations is possible through virtualization.

12.2 Disk-to-Disk-to-Tape (D2D2T)

Inserting an additional disk array into the disk-to-tape path may not seem like a particularly good idea from the standpoint of cost or simplification of management. Tape emulation, however, does offer substantial benefits in terms of performance, both for executing periodic tape backups and for retrieving archived data.

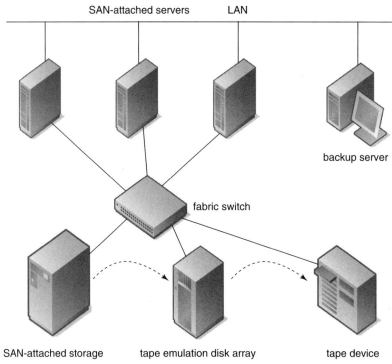

Figure 12.3 A secondary disk array may emulate a tape device to accelerate backup from the primary and provide responsive data recovery. For long-term storage, the tape emulation array spools the backup image to a physical tape library.

Originally used in mainframe environments, disk-to-disk-to-tape technology combines standard disk RAID functionality with a tape emulation application that can mimic the behavior of a variety of physical tape subsystems. As shown in Figure 12.3, a tape emulation disk array attaches to the SAN as another tape resource. Backup traffic may flow through a server or move through a third-party copy agent between the production array and the emulator. Tape backup applications communicate with tape devices to verify capability and to ensure that tape cartridges are loaded and available. With tape emulation, the specialty hardware posing as a tape device must respond to the tape backup application with the appropriate status characteristic of a specific tape unit. When a backup is launched, the data is written to back-end RAID disks, typically lower cost ATA drives. Depending on customer requirements, the data may secondarily be written from the tape emulator to a physical tape device or library. This provides transparency to the tape backup application while enabling significantly faster restore operations. Secondary archiving to physical tape provides long term storage on removable media that can be secured off-site.

Because tape emulation may span very different tape technologies, it is also possible to accommodate mixed environments for mainframe, midrange, and open systems applications. As illustrated in Figure 12.4, a single tape emulator may present different personalities to different host systems, as, for example, an IBM 3494 Enterprise Tape Library to an IBM OS/390 mainframe and a Quantum P7000 DLT (digital linear tape) device to an open-systems SAN. The tape backup applications in each environment communicate with the appropriate emulated tape device as data is actually written to disk. The physical tape system used for long-term storage may be yet another vendor brand—e.g., a StorageTek LTO (linear tape open) library.

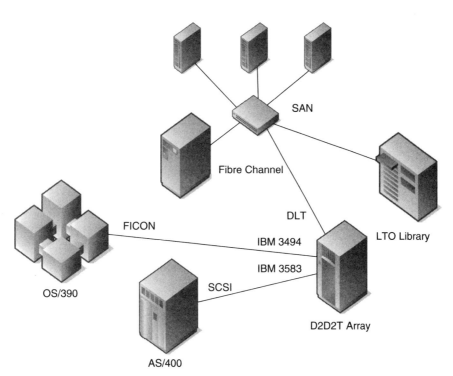

Figure 12.4 D2D2T technology facilitates tape emulation for a wide variety of host platforms and operating systems and enables more efficient utilization of large tape libraries.

Within open systems environments, disk-to-disk-to-tape emulation may be combined with virtualization of the storage systems that support production applications. Aside from providing various emulation modes for specific backup applications, though, D2D2T may compete with other virtualization services such as snapshots. A virtualization entity that supports snapshots also provides rapid data retrieval and the ability to save point-in-time copies to tape. For mixed mainframe and open systems environments, D2D2T is a viable means to consolidate tape backup operations while maintaining compatibility with existing backup applications and increasing both backup and recovery performance.

12.3 Virtualizing Tape Systems

Tape emulation on its own does not virtualize physical tape devices but simply substitutes one physical device for another. Like virtualization of storage disk systems, virtualization of tape systems requires an abstraction layer to create a virtual asset pool. Tape virtualization may be used to create a single logical view of a tape entity that is actually composed of multiple tape systems from different vendors or to present a single tape system as multiple logical tape drives. Some tape virtualization products are host-based, with the usual caveats of other host-based virtualization approaches. Other tape virtualization solutions are appliance-based and, like D2D2T, may support disk arrays for higher performance caching of tape backup streams as well as tape emulation to simulate different tape capabilities.

Tape virtualization leverages well-established disk technologies such as RAID to optimize performance and availability for long-term storage. Tape mirroring, for example, provides redundancy of tape images as a safeguard against data corruption or loss of a tape cartridge. Tape RAID is commonly referred to as RAIT (redundant array of independent tape devices) and in addition to mirroring may include striping of backup data across multiple physical tape systems. Large tape libraries may be combined into a tape pool for backup striping in the form of RAIL (redundant array of independent libraries). In addition, tape multicasting enables a single backup stream to be directed to two separate tape devices, typically separated by distance. A local tape backup, for example, can be simultaneously duplicated on a tape system at a geographically remote disaster recovery center.

As shown in Figure 12.5, storage virtualization of disk systems can be combined with tape virtualization for more flexible use of both disk and

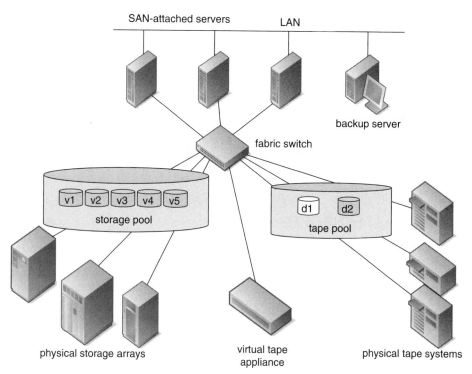

Figure 12.5 Through virtualization, multiple physical tape systems can be aggregated as a tape pool to increase performance and provide more efficient capacity utilization. Tape virtualization can be executed by host-based software or a SAN-attached virtual tape appliance.

tape assets. A storage pool presents virtual disks; a tape pool presents virtual tape devices. Although vendor proprietary features may be lost through abstraction, that loss may be an acceptable tradeoff for increased availability and flexibility in reassignment of tape assets. In this example, virtual disks may be backed up to virtual tape, either by conventional backup applications or through the intermediary of a third party copy agent. The diagram in Figure 12.5 does not specify where the storage virtualization occurs, e.g., in the fabric or through an appliance. Theoretically, a powerful virtualization engine could perform both disk array and tape library virtualization functions and provide a single point of management for configuring the entire virtualized environment.

Tape virtualization has also been extended to other long-term storage media such as optical storage. Traditionally, optical storage has been one of the last destinations for data through its lifecycle management. Optical storage's advantages in terms of capacity and immunity to electro-magnetic disturbance have been offset by its much slower performance compared to tape. Striping data across multiple optical storage systems helps overcome the performance stigma of optical technology and may make it a viable substitution for tape.

12.4 Chapter Summary

Conventional Tape Backup

■ LAN-based tape backup generates high traffic volumes on the LAN and is difficult to scale to large server populations.

■ Streamlining backup operations has been a prime motivation for SAN adoption.

■ SANs enable the consolidation of storage assets and centralized back operations over a high-performance network.

■ Third-party copy (TPC) removes the server from the backup data path.

■ A third-party copy agent may reside in a SAN switch, appliance, or tape device.

■ Tape systems may vary widely in capabilities, capacities, and tape formats.

Disk-to-Disk-to-Tape (D2D2T)

■ Tape emulation may use disk arrays to accelerate data backup and retrieval.

■ Tape emulation imitates the behavior of different tape systems and media handling.

■ The tape emulation agent should be transparent to upper layer backup applications.

■ Secondary archiving provides long-term storage on removable media that can be stored off-site.

■ D2D2T may provide emulation of tape systems for mainframe, midrange, and open systems platforms.

- D2D2T may compete with other virtualization services such as snapshots.

Virtualizing Tape Systems

- Tape virtualization enables creation of a tape pool of virtual tape devices.

- Tape virtualization may be host-based or appliance-based.

- RAIT (redundant array of independent tape devices) enables mirroring and data striping across multiple tape devices.

- RAIL (redundant array of independent libraries) enables RAID functions for large tape libraries.

- Tape multicasting facilitates simultaneous backup to both local and remote tape systems.

- Storage virtualization and tape virtualization may be combined to provide optimum utilization and performance for storage data.

- Virtualization of optical storage devices provides enhanced performance for long-term optical media storage.

13 Storage Automation and Virtualization

THE VIRTUALIZATION OF STORAGE systems has enabled useful services to optimize capacity utilization, provide high availability of storage data, overcome interoperability issues, and streamline storage administration. Storage pooling and use of auxiliary services such as data replication and snapshots are only the first step toward fully leveraging the potential of virtualization. This chapter examines emerging virtualization services that take storage administration to the next level by way of policy-based management and tighter integration between upper layer applications and virtualized storage.

13.1 Policy-Based Storage Management

Policy-based management is a broad category that encompasses a diversity of IT resources, including applications, computer platforms, networks, and storage. Policy-based management incorporates three basic elements: measurement of actual behavior, evaluation of that behavior against predefined rules or goals, and enforcement through behavior modification.

The common goal of policy management initiatives is to automate IT operations on the basis of specific criteria that align with higher level business requirements. Regulatory compliance, for example, may mandate that certain archived customer information be secured and confidential—and retrievable within 24 hours. Because this business obligation may only apply to a small portion of all data transactions, it is first necessary to identify which transactions are candidates for special treatment, and then to enforce data handling that meets the desired goals. Enforcement in this case may require a series of policies for linking specific applications to transport and data placement options and for dynamically manipulating physical devices to support those options. Policy definition may be provided by an upper layer management platform, but policy enforcement requires a tight integration of management and the complex environment of compute resources, network, and storage that supports data transactions. Ideally, this integration is provided by a common management interface that spans both management frameworks and a wide spectrum of infrastructure equipment.

The effort to define a common management interface for storage is being led by the Storage Networking Industry Association (SNIA). The SNIA Storage Management Interface Specification (SMI-S) is based on the common information model (CIM), which was originally developed by another industry group, the Desktop Management Task Force (DMTF). The DMTF had initially attempted to define a common management interface for desktop systems, but it soon became clear that common management should be extended to the entire network. Consequently, the DMTF became the Distributed Management Task Force, applying CIM to all networked assets.

CIM defines information models for interoperable management of network resources. Devices that support CIM can be monitored and managed uniformly by network management frameworks through a web-based enterprise management (WBEM) protocol. The CIM schema includes classes for defining policies and policy execution. In addition to the DMTF, the Internet Engineering Task Force (IETF) is also developing policy definitions for communications network management. The SNIA SMI-S technical workgroups have responsibility for storage and storage networking equipment CIM profile definitions overall, and the SNIA's Policy Work Group is concentrating on policy profiles specifically as they apply to storage.

Applying CIM/WBEM to storage HBAs, SAN switches, and storage devices requires creation of profiles with classes whose attributes reflect the unique capabilities of each type of product. A profile for a Fibre Channel switch, for example, may specify parameters for port statistics, device configuration, topology, and so on, regardless of manufacturer. Although this is useful for discovering and managing a particular device, the true power of SMI-S is in managing multiple switches, HBAs, and end devices as a single fabric entity that can in turn deliver higher level services such as optimized routing, zoning, and security for upper layer business applications.

SMI-S profiles for storage arrays began with common features such as RAID definition and LUN management, and have now been extended to storage virtualization through active management of storage pools, mirroring, and snapshots between storage systems. The CIM Schema, for example, now provides active management method calls such as CreateOrModify StoragePool( ) and CreateOrModifyElementFromStoragePool ( ) to generate and resize virtual pools and virtual volumes from them. The Storage Configuration Services of the DMTF CIM Schema will undergo further enhancement as the standard matures, bringing additional services under a common management that can leverage both virtualization and fabric shaping.

As shown in Figure 13.1, a successful CIM/WBEM implementation requires that physical devices such as HBAs, switches, storage arrays, and tape systems offer standards-compliant CIM providers for managing vendor-specific features as generic capabilities (although proxies may be available for the CIM-impaired). Techniques for configuring RAID levels, for example, may vary from vendor to vendor, but the CIM provider translates generic RAID configuration instructions from a CIM/WBEM management

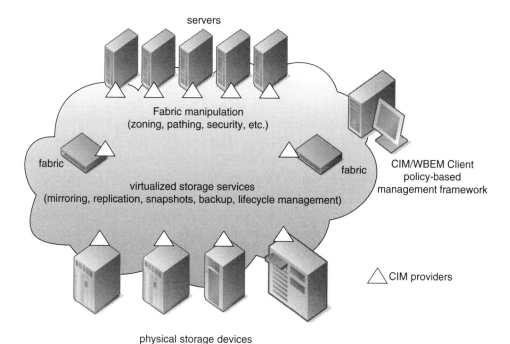

Figure 13.1 Homogeneous management of a heterogeneous SAN via CIM is provided by vendor-supplied CIM providers in all SAN components. Abstracting vendor proprietary capabilities into uniform vendor-neutral features enables the fabric and its storage assets to be treated as a single entity whose behavior is determined by higher level business requirements.

framework into the appropriate commands for a particular vendor's geometry. Likewise, the CIM Storage Configuration Services for creation and modification of storage pools may issue a generic command for creation of a pool of a specific size from multiple resources, which the CIM providers in each array execute in common. Because control using CIM encompasses both data transport and data placement, it is possible to manipulate both the fabric and its storage assets to accomplish a particular goal.

In combination with policy management, CIM services for fabrics and storage configuration enable dynamic manipulation of heterogeneous physical SAN assets via generic interface that can be tuned to specific business requirements. Through standardization, automation of storage operations can be established by a number of means, including upper layer management frameworks that supervise virtualized resources externally or embedded management intelligence that administers assets within the fabric. In either case, policy-based automation of storage is a major evolutionary step from management of physical devices within the SAN to management of the SAN itself as a virtualized resource supporting business requirements.

Creating a policy-based management scheme for storage is a complex undertaking. A policy for enforcing a certain quality of service level for a specific application, for example, may seem fairly straightforward, such as an online transaction processing application that requires high availability for data sets for a certain duration. Translating that policy into instructions that are ultimately supported by physical devices is far more difficult. Linking the policy to the application, for example, requires some means of identifying the application among all other applications that may be running on the SAN. Hopefully, the application is run on one or more dedicated servers, which can be identified through HBA World Wide Names and linked via fabric zoning to virtualized storage volumes on the back end. The virtual volumes, in turn, may be assigned to a particular class of storage, such as mirrored RAID 5 for high availability. Monitoring data status within those virtual volumes for lifecycle management, however, adds another layer of complexity and may require translation of file metadata for time stamp information to storage metadata for migration of blocks from high-availability storage to secondary storage over time. In addition, the association between the upper layer application and the various generations of data it has created must be maintained as the data sets migrate from one part of the SAN to another.

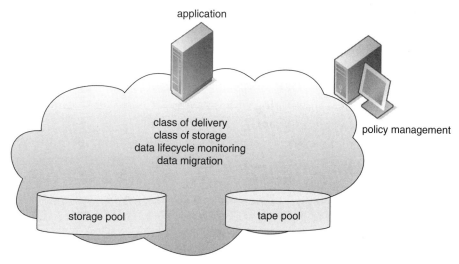

Figure 13.2 Policy-based management is predicated on a hierarchy of policy objects that govern different aspects of a virtualized infrastructure. Services under policy enforcement must be coordinated to accomplish the overall policy goal.

Policy-based management must also be flexible enough to accommodate changing business requirements as well as changes to the underlying infrastructure. Data archiving, for example, may be a phase of a particular policy for data handling. If the archive infrastructure is changed from disk-to-tape to disk-to-disk-to-tape, that change should be transparent to the upper layer application policy but recognized by lower layer policy objects that interface more directly with physical assets.

As shown in Figure 13.2, the layers of abstraction required for policy-based management transform the physical SAN into a collection of services under policy control. At this level, the physical connectivity of the SAN, pathing, zones, LUNs, and virtual volumes are transparent to policy definition. This requires considerable intelligence in the SAN in the form of sophisticated virtualization services and generic administration via CIM, but greatly simplifies day-to-day operation for business applications.

13.2 Application-Aware Storage Virtualization

Policy-based storage management requires the creation of a set of conditional policies that operate on lower level objects to achieve the desired results. Those policies, in turn, provide a foundation for building additional levels of abstraction to more closely integrate applications with virtualization services. Application-awareness assumes that the virtualization intelligence in the SAN has some means of identifying and automatically responding to specific requirements of individual applications. That identification may be very specific, such as analysis of frame content to recognize specific data types, or generic, such as simple monitoring of data traffic intensity to optimize fabric pathing and virtual volume expansion or contraction.

Policy-based management requires manual assignment of policies to specific servers or applications. Ideally, application-aware virtualization automates policy association and then implements additional policies as application behavior changes. An application-aware intelligence may index into transport data frames to identify a data type, such as streaming video, as shown in Figure 13.3. Having identified the particular application, the application-aware entity can then verify that the video stream data is being adequately serviced, depending on policies already established for that data type. In this instance, video data is best supported by very high performance storage, ideally written to the outer, longer tracks of multiple physical disks. If the video application is not already assigned to this class of storage, the application-aware intelligence should be able to engage the appropriate

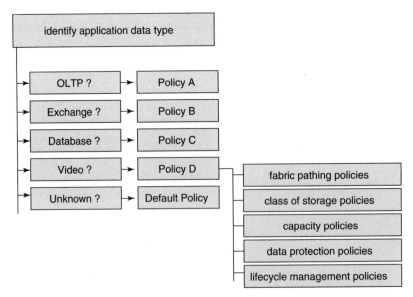

Figure 13.3 Application-aware virtualization requires identification of the upper layer application based on data characteristics and enforcement of a policy hierarchy to apply the appropriate storage services over time.

storage virtualization services to reassign the application to a higher class of storage and perform any data migration required for the new virtual volume. In addition, pathing through the fabric may be adjusted to meet throughput requirements such as bursty traffic conditions that may require load balancing. Thereafter, an application-aware entity may monitor the capacity requirements of the upper layer application, automatically resizing virtual volumes to fully maximize capacity utilization over time.

Application-awareness for storage virtualization is a variation on the theme established by application-aware (layer 7) routers and switches in IP networking environments. Like those products, application-aware storage virtualization entities must be able to perform frame cracking and policy enforcement at wire-speed. Unlike those products, however, storage applications are less readily identified than TCP/IP-based applications, and thus present a much greater challenge for automated servicing.

Given the high-performance requirements for frame monitoring and decoding, an application-aware virtualization engine is best positioned where centralized wire-speed frame handling already occurs, i.e., within a fabric switch or optimized in-band appliance. Once an application data type has been recognized, the fabric or appliance may interact with other management frameworks to initiate the appropriate policies for data handling and placement.

13.3 Virtualization-Aware Applications

Another approach to application and virtualization integration is provided by the introduction of virtualization-sensitive controls within the upper layer applications themselves. This is facilitated by virtualization-enabled features within the supporting operating system, such as Microsoft's support of virtual volumes, snapshots, and alternate pathing within Windows 2000. Virtualization awareness within applications simplifies the task of linking applications to storage policy enforcement, since the application itself can inform the virtualized SAN as to its specific transport and data handling requirements.

As shown in Figure 13.4, initial storage services requirements—such as availability, class of storage, and archiving—may be communicated to the SAN via configuration parameters that are loaded as the application establishes its connection to the SAN. Those parameters may be processed by the operating system, which in turn leverages the appropriate APIs to commu-

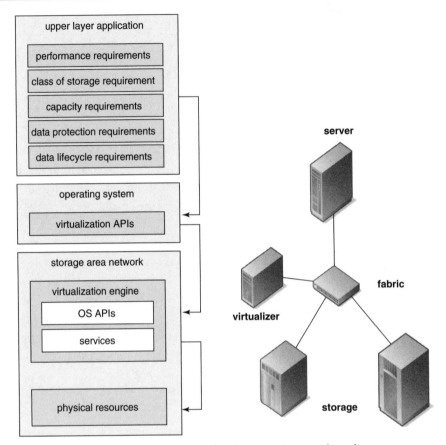

Figure 13.4 A virtualization-aware application may communicate its requirements to the operating system virtualization APIs, which in turn notifies the SAN-based virtualization engine. This configuration puts the application in control of its supporting storage infrastructure.

nicate with a SAN-based virtualization entity. For day-to-day operations, the application may monitor its own capacity requirements and initiate dynamic volume resizing or flag records or files for data aging and thus trigger lifecycle management policies.

Compared to application-aware virtualization, virtualization-awareness by applications extends storage intelligence beyond the SAN and provides a more holistic integration of applications and infrastructure. Instead of reverse-engineering application needs via frame cracking, the application itself can proactively manipulate the storage environment to suit its own purposes.

13.4 Chapter Summary

Policy-Based Storage Management

- Policy-based management encompasses all IT resources, including applications, computer platforms, networks, and storage.

- Policy management is necessary for aligning underlying technology to business requirements.

- The SNIA Storage Management Interface Specification (SMI-S) establishes a common management structure for heterogeneous SANs.

- The common information model (CIM) defines management objects for a wide diversity of network and compute resources.

- CIM objects are managed through the web-based enterprise management (WBEM) protocol.

- The CIM Schema includes policy classes for automating IT processes.

- CIM provides a Storage Configuration Service model for creating and manipulating virtualized resources.

- CIM storage services and policy objects may be combined to provide automated storage virtualization.

- Policy management is based on a hierarchy of policies that span from upper layer interfaces to underlying physical resources.

- Policy-based management transforms the physical SAN into a collection of services supporting business application requirements.

Application-Aware Storage Virtualization

- Policy-based management provides a foundation for tighter integration of applications and storage virtualization.

- An application-aware virtualization entity must identify specific application data types and launch the appropriate policies for data handling.

- Application-aware virtualization must respond to changing application needs, such as capacity requirements and lifecycle management.

- Wire-speed frame analysis is required to maintain storage performance levels.

Virtualization-Aware Applications

■ Virtualization APIs with an operating system enable upper layer applications to communicate requirements to storage virtualization entities in the SAN.

■ Virtualization-awareness facilitates the integration of applications and infrastructure by enabling the application to define its own storage requirements.

■ Virtualization-aware applications expand the scope of storage intelligence beyond the SAN .

14

The Storage Utility

THE EVOLUTION OF STORAGE VIRTUALIZATION from the abstraction of physical disks to the abstraction of entire storage systems, and from rudimentary services such as mirroring, replication, and snapshots to automated and policy-based management, has been dependent on the pace of development of basic SAN technology. The plumbing had to be in place and operational before high-level services could be added. This final chapter reviews the current status of storage virtualization solutions and useful storage services that are emerging on that foundation.

14.1 Dependencies

The storage networking industry continues to generate new technologies. Some are based on the dialectic between vendors and customers as customers feed business requirements into vendor product planning. Others are based on successive advances in technology that enable new functionality not previously conceivable until a critical mass of capabilities is reached. In the former category, customer input has driven interoperability and management as priorities for SAN development. In the latter case, IP SAN technology was driven by the widespread adoption of Gigabit Ethernet and the feasibility of running block storage over IP at speeds suitable for business applications.

For customers, the notion of simplifying storage administration via a storage utility model that was articulated by the Compaq ENSA document in 2000 has always been attractive, but delivering the technology to make this possible has been dependent on technical advances in diverse SAN-related areas. The reliability and transparency inherent in a utility are dependent on advances in interoperability, management, performance, security, data protection, multi-protocol support, and higher levels of integration of storage awareness with operating systems and applications. These things take time. In the meantime, storage customers have businesses to run and will cautiously adopt new functionality in increments as the benefits and reliability of new solutions are proven in practice.

Interoperability sometimes drives vendors into bipolar disorder. Interoperability of SAN devices is mandatory for market penetration if for no other reason than that customers often have no particular vendor loyalty and insist on buying products that suit their particular business needs from various sources. Vendors are expected to adapt to this behavior, which results in long compatibility matrices and considerable investment by vendors in interoperability testing and certification.

On the other hand, open systems interoperability is always at odds with vendor proprietary value-add, the unique functionality that makes products competitive in the market. If all products are interoperable and provide only the same standardized features, market differentiation devolves to price. That is a short-term benefit for customers, but ultimately undermines technical innovation. In the storage networking industry, interoperability between fabric switches, between HBAs in the same environment, between storage targets, and between SAN applications has been a difficult accomplishment. But although more progress on interoperability is needed, the current state of SAN interoperability is sufficient for supporting reliable multi-vendor storage networks and this has been an essential premise for the development of storage virtualization. A virtualization entity must be able to communicate with a diversity of host and storage assets in a common open systems vocabulary.

Along with interoperability, management of SANs has been a persistent issue for customers and an inhibitor to more widespread SAN adoption. Unfortunately, management of products typically lags behind product deployment. In the case of SAN technology, resolving physical transport issues and protocols achieving stability for storage applications have been the highest priorities, with management initially limited to device configuration and monitoring. In a multi-vendor SAN, that meant supporting multiple management workstations with separate device managers for HBAs, disk arrays, tape devices, and fabric switches. Although high-level management frameworks were developed to monitor SAN components with SNMP, there was no single pane of glass solution for active management of all devices or manage storage assets across vendor lines. Currently, a number of management frameworks are sufficiently comprehensive to monitor and re-configure SAN devices and assets, but standardization via the SNIA SMIS initiative is required to more closely align storage management with customer requirements. No customer particularly enjoys configuring minutiae on a complex of discrete products simply in order to enable overall high availability or data protection within the SAN. The maturation of SAN management from management of devices to management of broader business objectives is thus another prerequisite for the further development of storage virtualization.

Performance has been another gating factor for virtualization. Few customers will sacrifice performance in production environments to achieve an additional benefit. For the SAN infrastructure, the evolution of Fibre Channel through 1 Gbps, 2 Gbps, 4 Gbps, and 10 Gbps transport speeds continually raises the bar for performance of other SAN components. Host systems typically do not need the multi-gigabit enhancements, but implanting higher speeds on storage ports and fabric switches enables a greater fan-in ratio of servers to storage and the construction of high-performance core fabrics for aggregating 1000s of devices in a storage network. For storage virtualization, high performance in data transport is both a dependency and a liability. Higher performance in the SAN infrastructure provides greater efficiency for virtualization services such as mirroring and data replication between storage systems. Higher performance also mandates, however, that the virtualization entity has sufficient processing power and memory to handle multiple concurrent block address mapping transactions at multi-gigabit wire speeds. For in-band appliances and intelligent switches in particular, ASIC-based virtualization is required to cope with the potential load that a multi-gigabit transport imposes.

Security, like SAN management, is another service that has trailed behind SAN adoption. In part, the lack of security options for SANs was due to the physical isolation of most storage networks in data centers as well as the use of Fibre Channel, which had no history of malevolent snooping or protocol hacking. The more widespread adoption of SANs in departments and branches and the introduction of IP-based SAN products has focused attention on the vulnerabilities of storage networks to both operator error and intentional capture of sensitive storage data. In the past few years, vendors have enhanced their security offerings by providing authentication protocols for management interfaces and data encryption for data in flight across the network and data at rest on disk or tape. In addition, security can be enforced within the fabric through port binding (only allowing authorized devices to attach to specific ports) and fabric binding (only allowing designated switches to be connected in a common fabric). Likewise, SAN routing can enforce authorized connectivity for storage devices between separate SANs while isolating faults that may cause disruption from SAN to SAN. Collectively, the security features that have been created for storage networking complement the implementation of storage virtualization. The ability to pool storage assets and dynamically allocate capacity and classes of storage to specific applications has more value when the data and the infrastructure it traverses are secured.

Data protection in the form of mirroring, replication, snapshot, and tape archiving technologies has also matured over time to provide richer functionality. Simple mirroring between two storage arrays has been supplemented by three- or multiple-way mirroring, active/active mirroring, and use of secondary mirrors to expedite nondisruptive back operations. Data replication over distance has evolved to support both longer distances for synchronous replication and much higher latencies for asynchronous replication. Data protection of entire volumes or arrays has been enhanced with point-in-time snapshots that provide the ability to quickly restore transactions to a known good point in time. Last, although tape technology has not been in the vanguard of SAN technical development, today's products and backup software offer higher performance, greater capacity, and flexibility through integration with disk (e.g., D2D2T) and management applications (e.g., data lifecycle management). These technical improvements make the application of storage virtualization services far more productive for customers and enable new storage strategies that were inconceivable a few years ago.

In terms of multi-protocol support, SAN infrastructure and applications that were nurtured on Fibre Channel are now adapting to iSCSI, iFCP, and FCIP to extend the reach of block storage data over distance and encompass larger populations of servers. Multi-protocol block data transport over IP provides many benefits unachievable with Fibre Channel alone. Fibre Channel is still a relatively expensive technology and presents a barrier to entry for inexpensive servers. As it turns out, large enterprises that run their most mission-critical applications on Fibre Channel have hundreds or thousands of these lower end servers. Each server that is not connected to shared storage represents additional administrative costs. iSCSI and iSCSI gateways are enabling customers to further reduce operational costs and streamline storage and backup operations for all servers. In addition, SAN routing and iFCP are enabling multi-protocol integration of SANs and IP while eliminating issues such as broadcast storms and fabric reconfigurations. The ability to reliably span Fibre Channel, Ethernet, and IP networks for storage transactions gives storage virtualization a much greater scope and enables asset sharing across the enterprise.

Finally, the shift of storage from direct-attached to network-attached storage was predicated on transparency between the operating system SCSI I/O and the changed storage environment. This was not accomplished without some difficulty, though, since behavior in a shared configuration is necessarily different than behavior in a dedicated configuration. LUN masking and zoning were therefore required within the fabric to enforce orderly attachment to shared assets. Subsequently, features such as alternate pathing and failover required SAN awareness on the part of the operating system, and that awareness has now been extended to SAN-based services such as shadow copies and storage pooling. APIs that enable interaction between upper layer applications and the SAN infrastructure mark a further advance in storage networking and the more productive use of storage virtualization services.

Current SAN capabilities have demonstrated sufficient stability and end-user value that all enterprise networks are now running their most critical business applications on SANs. This success has helped fund new technical innovations as vendors attempt to more fully exploit the opportunities that shared storage networking generates. Further improvements in interoperability, management, performance, security, multi-protocol support, and application/storage integration are driving more functionality into storage virtualization. At the same time, storage virtualization is propelling those improvements as customers begin to demand more from their vendors.

14.2 Enabling the Storage Utility

The ultimate success of a technology is demonstrated by its ubiquity. A few decades ago, information technology was dependent on monolithic mainframe processing that only large enterprises could afford. User access via unintelligent terminals was restricted to business applications running on the central processor. Control of those applications and their data was centralized in the data center, with departments completely dependent on data center programmers for how data was processed and presented. And although communication networks existed, they stood in isolation from one another, with transactions between companies conducted via paper documents. Today, information technology is ubiquitous. Data processing has been decentralized, information workers use intelligent PCs with more processing power than the previous generation mainframes, applications and data are under departmental control, and business networks are interconnected through the global Internet. Ubiquity of information technology has spread beyond business use to personal use, and access to a wealth of information on the Internet is readily available in schools, public libraries, and the home. That is success.

Ubiquitous adoption, however, is not possible without simplification of the user interface and commoditizing of the technology. For customers, simpler and cheaper are good. For vendors, simplification helps sell more products, but commoditizing sources of profit is never a good idea. The success of a technology is therefore under a profound geologic stress as vendors attempt to meet customer demands for efficiency, simplification and lower cost while maintaining margins with additional value-added features and greater volumes of product shipments.

Storage networking technology has established its success within large enterprises, but is only now beginning to spread to the broad medium and small business market. Although ubiquitous adoption for business applications is assured by the proven benefits of shared storage solutions, further market penetration on the scale of PCs and Internet access may take time. It might be nice, for example, to share TIVO'ed programs with friends and neighbors via a personal IP SAN, but that implies affordability of both the SAN technology and satellite services on a broader scale than today.

The introduction of iSCSI, modular shared storage based on inexpensive disks, and basic storage virtualization functionality for automating capacity allocation and data handling is creating new classes of connectivity and classes of storage for both the mid-tier market and large enterprises. This does not mean, however, that large enterprises will forklift their existing Fibre Channel SANs in favor of inexpensive ones. The new storage technologies that are enabling SANs to become more ubiquitous in the broader market are also driving more ubiquity into every corner of large enterprise networks. Using storage virtualization to simplify operations for high-end storage systems and servers has value, but applying storage virtualization technology to a wide spectrum of classes of storage and classes of servers within the enterprise has far more value.

As referenced in Chapter 1, the SNIA virtualization taxonomy divides storage virtualization into three basic aspects: what is being virtualized, where is the virtualizing being done, and how is it being done. From a customer perspective, what is being virtualized depends on the applications used to support business goals. Virtualizing block data access in the form of storage pooling may be sufficient for some enterprises; virtualizing file systems as well may be required for others. The where and how of virtualization, however, are simply technical issues that, given comparable performance, reliability, and transparency, are a matter of customer preference. Host-based virtualization may be suitable for some customers, while network-based virtualization is preferred by others. Certainly, the choice between in-band and out-of-band virtualization methods is a toss-up, given that both have demonstrated adequate performance for business applications. In the end, customer preference will be reinforced by the degree of integration between virtualization products and other advanced services such as CIM-based policy management and virtualization-aware APIs within operating systems and applications.

The ultimate goal of storage virtualization is to facilitate a storage utility that fully abstracts the physical existence of the SAN transport and underlying storage resources. How would the storage utility work? It might work something like this:

A customer attaches a new server running a new application to the storage network. If it is an iSCSI server, the server registers its presence with an iSNS (Internet Storage Name Server) server at a well-known IP address, authenticates itself with a digital signature and negotiates the appropriate IPSec (IP Security) protocols for security and data encryption. If it is a Fibre Channel server, the server authenticates itself to the Fibre Channel fabric, which may use access control lists (ACLs), port binding, or other mechanisms to grant connectivity. The multi-switch fabric itself is secured through fabric binding to prevent unauthorized connection of other switches. With either iSCSI or Fibre Channel, the security protocols employed ensure that the new server is an authorized participant in the SAN, based on pre-established security policies managed via CIM/WBEM.

Having registered its presence and attributes with the SAN, the server may query the storage network for available storage resources. Through virtualization APIs, the fabric may communicate with the virtualization entity within the SAN to provide a virtual volume for the server's use. The size of that virtual volume may be a default storage allocation, which in turn

can be modified on the fly to accommodate greater or lesser storage requirements for the application. The virtual volume itself is drawn from the storage pool, which may span multiple heterogeneous storage systems.

So far, the secure connection to the storage network and initial storage
allocation has occurred in isolation from the upper layer application. When
the application loads, it may inform the storage network of its specific
requirements, e.g., class of storage, capacity, availability, performance, security, lifecycle management, and other parameters. Based on policy management, the storage network creates the appropriate resources for assignment
to the server. If the application is not virtualization-aware, the storage network may assign default data handling policies and then monitor the application storage traffic to identify specific data types that could be subject to
other policies.

For day-to-day operations, the storage network constantly monitors the
I/Os between the server and its designated resources. As activity increases,
for example, the SAN may respond with traffic shaping policies to enhance
performance. As capacity utilization increases or decreases, the SAN may re-
allocate data blocks to meet application needs as well as optimize utilization
of the storage pool. The application itself may mark specific data for lifecycle management so that the data may be migrated to secondary storage tiers
and then to tape, or the SAN may monitor access frequency to determine
whether data is subject to specific lifecycle policies. Likewise, an application's security status may change over time, requiring automatic migration of
its volumes to assets that provide data encryption for disk or tape.

On the back end, virtualization services for high-availability storage
have been automatically generated. If, for example, a new array is attached
to the storage network, virtualization intelligence automatically identifies it,
categorizes it by class of storage, and assigns it to the storage pool for collective use. If a new tape library is connected, the virtualization intelligence
may assign it to a virtual tape pool or integrate it into an existing disk-to-
disk-to-tape configuration.

As more servers and applications are added to the SAN, virtualization
services may accumulate utilization and performance statistics to proactively generate trend analysis reports to notify the administrator when additional physical assets should be added to the storage pool or when
additional load-sharing links should be added to the network infrastructure.
Utilization statistics can also be used to feed billing applications so that departments are appropriately billed for their storage usage based on class of
service requirements.

From the administrator's standpoint, the new server was simply attached to the SAN and all the appropriate storage services were automatically enabled: No manual configuration of the fabric switch, no manual creation and assignment of LUNs, no manual definition of security parameters, no manual configuration of mirroring or data replication, no monitoring of utilization to avoid "out of disk space" faults, and no manual configuration of backups. In the storage utility ideal, all of these manual processes are handled by intelligence in the storage network.

Like electrical or other service utilities, however, the simplicity of connection to the service is predicated on considerable complexity within the service infrastructure. At some point, generation plants and substations were built, workers hung power lines, loads were defined and operational requirements established. When a transformer blows, someone has to go out and fix it. Likewise, the initial creation of a storage utility may require significant manual configuration. Common management APIs through CIM/WBEM will streamline this process, because it enables intelligence within individual products to communicate with intelligence in management frameworks that can, in turn, apply policies to determine how those products will be used.

Although the storage utility may still be some years off, the enabling foundation of storage virtualization is already being built. Vendors and customers alike have affirmed the value of reliable and transparent storage services, and initiatives such as FAIS and the SNIA SMI-S are raising the IQ of the SAN. When the storage utility is finally in place, though, it will not be an obvious event accompanied by ribbon cutting and banging of drums. It will be the result of a steady introduction of enhanced virtualization and management services that gradually automate manual processes and enable technology itself to handle its own underlying complexity.

14.3 Chapter Summary

Dependencies
- Storage networking technology is driven by both customer requirements and accumulated advances in technical capabilities.

- Attainment of a storage utility is dependent on further progress in interoperability, management, performance, security, data protection, multiprotocol support, and alignment of storage virtualization and applications.

■ Interoperability between SAN switches, HBAs, and storage targets is a precondition for the logical abstraction of heterogeneous SAN assets.

■ Standardized management of storage transport and data placement must extend from management of physical devices to management of business objectives.

■ Higher performance in the SAN requires higher performance of virtualization engines.

■ SAN security features enable virtualization to safely allocate storage assets to authorized servers.

■ Advances in data protection techniques provide more powerful tools for virtualization services, such as lifecycle management.

■ Multi-protocol support gives storage virtualization a greater scope in sharing storage assets across the enterprise.

■ Tighter integration between applications, operating systems, and storage virtualizers aligns data transport and placement with application needs.

Enabling the Storage Utility

■ The ultimate success of a technology is demonstrated by its ubiquity.

■ Ubiquitous adoption is predicated on simplification of the user interface and commoditizing of the technology.

■ New storage technologies such as iSCSI and inexpensive modular storage are driving broader market penetration for SANs.

■ The value of storage virtualization is enhanced by encompassing more classes of servers and classes of storage within the enterprise.

■ Where storage virtualization is done and how it is executed is less important than what services are provided.

■ The ultimate goal of storage virtualization is to facilitate storage as a utility.

■ Simplification of storage administration requires the application of technology to overcome its own complexity.

Appendix A
Industry Resources

Storage Virtualization Industry Resources

http://www.snia.org/education/tutorials

(Tutorials on virtualization and SMIS)

http://www.snia.org/education/dictionary

(Virtualization and storage networking terminology)

http://www.fibrechannel.org/

(Vendor-supplied material from the Fibre Channel Industry Association)

http://sunsite.berkeley.edu/TechRepPages/CSD-87-391

(original Berkeley RAID proposal)

Standards and Proposals

SCSI and Fibre Channel Standards

www.T10.org

(ANSI T10 Technical Committee)

www.T11.org

(ANSI T11 Technical Committee with links to T11.5 and FAIS)

www.cern.ch/HSI/FCS

(European Laboratory for Particle Physics)

CIM/WBEM

www.dmtf.org/standards

(DMTF CIM/WBEM Standards)

IETF Requests for Comments
www.ietf.org
(Internet Engineering Task Force)

ftp://ftp.isi.edu/in-notes
(University of Southern CA School of Engineering Information
Sciences)

Gigabit Ethernet
http://standards.ieee.org
(IEEE Standards site)

www.manta.ieee.org/groups/802/3/
(IEEE Ethernet Working Group)

Appendix B
Vendor Resources

Product	Web Site URL
Storage Virtualization Software and Appliances	
Computer Associates	www.ca.com
DataCore	www.datacore.com
FalconStor	www.falconstor.com
Netreon	www.netreon.com
SANRAD	www.sanrad.com
StoneFly Networks	www.stonefly.com
StoreAge	www.store-age.com
Tivoli	www.tivoli.com
VERITAS Software	www.veritas.com
Vicom	www.vicom.com
Virtualization-Enabled Storage Systems	
Compellent	www.compellent.com
EMC	www.emc.com
Hewlett-Packard	www.hp.com
Hitachi Data Systems	www.hds.com
IBM	www.ibm.com
Network Appliance	www.netapp.com
Overland Data	www.overlanddata.com
StorageTek	www.network.com

Product	Web Site URL

Virtualization-Enabled Storage Systems (*cont.*)

Sun Microsystems	www.sun.com
XIOtech	www.xiotech.com

SAN System Vendors (servers, interconnect, storage)

Avid (video)	www.avid.com
Bull	www.bull.com
Dell	www.dell.com
Fujitsu	www.ftsi.fujitsu.com
Hewlett-Packard	www.hp.com
IBM	www.ibm.com
NEC	www.nec.com
Sun	www.sun.com
Unisys	www.unisys.com

SAN Storage and Tape Vendors

ADIC	www.adic.com
DotHill	www.dothill.com
Ciprico	www.ciprico.com
Compellent	www.compellent.com
DataDirect	www.datadirectnetworks.com
Dell Computers	www.dell.com
EMC	www.emc.com
Eurologic	www.eurologic.com
Exabyte	www.exabyte.com
Hewlett-Packard	www.hp.com
Hitachi Data Systems	www.hds.com
IBM	www.ibm.com
LSI	www.lsilogic.com

Product	Web Site URL
MTI	www.mti.com
Network Appliance	www.netapp.com
Overland Data	www.overlanddata.com
Procom	www.procom.com
Quantum	www.quantum.com
Raidtec	www.raidtec.com
Siemens	www.sni.com
SpectraLogic	www.spectralogic.com
StorageTek	www.network.com
Sun Microsystems	www.sun.com
Unisys	www.unisys.com
XIOtech	www.xiotech.com

Fibre Channel Interconnect Products

Adaptec	www.adaptec.com
Agilent	www.agilent.com
ATTO Technology	www.attotech.com
Brocade	www.brocade.com
Cisco Systems	www.cisco.com
Crossroads	www.crossroads.com
Emulex	www.emulex.com
Hewlett-Packard	www.hp.com
IBM	www.ibm.com
JNI	www.jni.com
LSI Logic	www.lsilogic.com
McDATA	www.mcdata.com
Qlogic	www.qlogic.com
Troika Networks	www.troikanetworks.com

Product	Web Site URL
IP SAN Products	
Adaptec	www.adaptec.com
Agilent	www.agilent.com
Alacritech	www.alacritech.com
Cisco	www.cisco.com
Emulex	www.emulex.com
Falconstor	www.falconstor.com
Hewlett-Packard	www.hp.com
Hitachi Data Systems	www.hds.com
IBM	www.ibm.com
Intel	www.intel.com
JNI	www.jni.com
Lucent	www.lucent.com
Maranti Networks	www.marantinetworks.com
McDATA	www.mcdata.com
Qlogic	www.qlogic.com
SANRAD	www.sanrad.com
Spectra Logic	www.spectralogic.com
StoneFly Networks	www.stoneflynetworks.com
Trebia	www.trebia.com
Troika Networks	www.troikanetworks.com
XIOTech	www.xiotech.com
SAN Extension	
AT&T	www.att.com
Brocade	www.brocade.com
CNT	www.cnt.com
Lucent	www.lucent.com
McDATA	www.mcdata.com
Nortel	www.nortelnetworks.com

Product	Web Site URL
SAN Management	
BakBone Software	www.bakbone.com
BMC	www.bmc.com
CommVault	www.commvault.com
Computer Associates	www.ca.com
CreekPath	www.creekpath.com
Data Direct	www.datadirect.com
EMC	www.emc.com
Hitachi Data Systems	www.hds.com
KOM Networks	www.komnetworks.com
Legato Systems	www.legato.com
Maranti Networks	www.marantinetworks.com
McDATA	www.mcdata.com
Netreon	www.netreon.com
Sun Microsystems	www.sun.com
Tivoli	www.tivoli.com
VERITAS Software	www.veritas.com
Vicom	www.vicom.com
Gigabit Ethernet Vendors	
Avaya	www.avaya.com
Avici Systems	www.avici.com
Cisco	www.cisco.com
Extreme	www.extremenetworks.com
Foundry	www.foundrynetworkd.com
Juniper	www.juniper.net
Nortel	www.nortelnetworks.com
RiverStone	www.riverstonenetworks.com
Test Equipment and Verification Labs	
Ancot	www.ancot.com

Product	Web Site URL

Test Equipment and Verification Labs (*cont.*)

Product	Web Site URL
Finisar	www.finisar.com
Imation Labs	www.imation.com
I-Tech	www.i-tech.com
Medusa Labs	www.medusalabs.com
Mier Communications	www.mier.com
Network Associates	www.sniffer.com
SNIA Technology Center	www.snia.org
Solution Technology	www.soltechnology.com
Tek-Tools	www.tek-tools.com
Xyratex	www.xyratex.com

Appendix C
Observations and Speculations

I'VE PROVIDED THIS APPENDIX to give industry observers, analysts, technologists, and customers an opportunity to express their views on storage virtualization and its future capabilities. The observations vary considerably, as one might expect, given the broad circumference of the subject and its impact on diverse aspects of data storage.

Delivering a Global Storage Solution

Gary Johnson

SAN Architect

Carlson Companies

At Carlson we see virtualization as being the cornerstone for several indicatives. First is the ability to manipulate and manage storage while it remains available to the production environment. We have designed a new backup/recovery environment with this capability in mind. Using virtualization of storage we will take snapshots of a primary disk on servers. A copy of that snapshot will be made in the backup/recovery environment. That disk copy will be used for recovery of files and or servers. Data will be copied to tape for offsite purposes. Snapshots and replication will be managed at a sector and block level, ensuring the efficient use of network and storage resources. This new backup environment will facilitate a serverless backup. Since the replication is sector and block level delta it will also be feasible and efficient to replicate the data to a different facility.

In fact, the primary driver for us to use this technology is to allow a central IT organization to manage storage at a remote location. This removes the burden of backup and recovery of IT systems from the staff at remote locations, allowing them to employ the proper resources to serve the business at those locations.

The second initiative is to facilitate Information Life Cycle Management. Traditionally, to get the right data, on the right storage, at the right price, we have either had an expensive disk subsystem or direct-attached storage. We are now looking to build three to four storage tiers with different performance characteristics, different SLAs, and of course different price points. Storage virtualization will facilitate the movement of data between these tiers of storage, as well as clarify the policies defining what and when data should be moved between tiers. Information Life Cycle Management has as much to do with process as technology, but virtualization enables it.

Along with the ability to move the data to the proper storage, virtualization will also enable better disk utilization. Again, being able to manipulate the physical storage without impacting the logical presentation of storage to servers is very important. Virtualization almost always allows for the dynamic expansion of a LUN; some allow for reducing the LUN size. The ability to dynamically grow a LUN on the fly considerably reduces the disk requirements, especially when you consider the a typical database where you may have a production copy plus two or three copies for backup, plus a QA instance and a Dev instance. With virtualization storage tiers, the production instance may reside on the most expensive disk, but the copies for backup could reside on the least expensive disk with QA and Dev on the middle tier of disk. Thus, increasing disk utilization and getting the data on the right disk tier will result in a more efficient environment.

Storage virtualization is the enabling technology for Carlson to deliver a Global Storage Solution that is cost effective, efficient, highly available, and flexible enough to meet the business requirements.

Virtualizing Servers, Storage, and Networks

Greg Schulz

Senior Analyst, The Evaluator Group

Author of *Resilient Storage Networks* (Elsevier)

For anyone using computers, video games, cell phones, PDAs, or the Internet, virtualization is all around us. The concept of Cyberspace in itself is a form of masking the real and physical from the abstract. Yet hidden and unseen are the real and physical infrastructure items that exist to support these virtual environments. Within this real and physical infrastructure are applications, servers, telecommunications networks, and storage, supported by people who configure, manage, and take care of them. A key attribute of any form of virtualization is transparency and ease of deployment. Virtualization technologies serve to mask, abstract, and transparently leverage underlying resources without applications and consumers having to understand or know how to use the physical attributes of the resource. For example, virtual tape in the IBM Mainframe environment, known as virtual tape library (VTL) and virtual tape systems (VTS), utilize virtualization techniques to adapt different technology to be used by existing tape processing functions and software with simplicity. Another example is that some older legacy applications still think they are processing 80-column punch cards when in reality they are being accessed via sophisticated JAVA- and XML-based GUIs, which is a form of virtual I/O to adapt something old to something new. Even more amazing is when these legacy programs have been moved from a mainframe to a desktop or laptop computer.

Some other areas where virtualization technology and techniques are being used are virtual disk—for example, a LUN or partition on a RAID storage subsystem and virtual I/O devices. Volume managers and file systems also implement virtualization techniques to aggregate (pool) and provide a layer of abstraction between real physical and virtual resources for transparent access of storage by applications. Other functions that are often grouped under the umbrella of storage virtualization include mirroring and remote data replication, long distance data access support, wide area file services (WAFS), data movement and migration, security, and protocol conversion.

Telephone networks are a good example of a virtual network and resource in that you can use cell phones to talk to a traditional "land-based" telephone, you call and talk to someone in the United States from elsewhere in the world, and you connect your PC into a phone line for dialup access to the Internet when high-speed access is not available. The same network can be used for moving voice, video, and data, including faxes over wireless, copper, and fiber optic cabling. In some instances you might need an adapter cord, plug, or interface module; however, you can access and utilize the transparent, virtual resources of the underlying physical telephone network.

A virtual storage network similar to a telephone network supports many different interfaces—for example, Fibre Channel, Ethernet, InfiniBand,

SATA, SAS, SONET/SDH, and others, as well as multiple protocols including SCSI, FCP, iSCSI, FCIP, iFCP, TCP/IP, iSER, and others. A virtual storage network can also support access via Block-, File- (NAS), and Object-based to meet the different needs of applications and adapt to support different technology resources. Like the telephone network, you may need special plugs, adapters, or connectors to access and use a storage network. Standard interfaces and protocols are needed and continue to evolve to leverage storage virtualization, including SMI-S and FAIS as well as others being worked on by IETF, ANSI T11, SNIA, DMTF, and DAT collaborative, among others.

Not so long ago, a major discussion point was the convergence of block and file, also known as SAN and NAS. We are now seeing the convergence of servers and storage, which is only appropriate given discussion of virtual servers and virtual storage. While storage virtualization services continue to be deployed on servers and storage subsystems, they are also being deployed in the network on appliances, switches, and gateways.

A barrier to fully leveraging virtual servers, virtual storage, and virtual networks may not be technology, but rather political and budget boundaries, as well as "turf" wars within organizations. Even with organizations continuing to run and be organized as they are, there are benefits from improved resource usage and improved management that can be realized by server, storage, and network virtualization, as we have seen over past several years.

So the next time you access a web page, perform a Google search, hit the return key on a website, or perform some other function using your computer, pause for a moment to think about what makes up cyberspace. While it may seem like a virtual environment, keep in mind that there is a real infrastructure of servers, storage, and networks that have been virtualized to enable you not to have to worry about the technologies that exist to enable you to do what you need to do.

Moving Storage Virtualization Up the Stack

Paul Massiglia

Technical Director Foundation Technical Product Management

VERITAS Software Corporation

Storage virtualization is a solved problem.

To be sure, there are still some messy details to clean up. The SNIA's Storage Management Initiative, with all the tremendous progress it has made, still has challenges lying before it. Using virtual storage isn't as easy as we'd like it to be. But as an industry, we fundamentally know how to virtualize storage. We can create virtual devices with an impressive variety of cost, performance, and availability characteristics, using the facilities of storage systems, intelligent storage network switches, and host-based virtualization software. Using storage network facilities, we can make virtual devices available to some servers and block access to them from others and re-provision devices to other servers when requirements change. Over the last decade, we've brought Fibre Channel networks from birth to maturity and followed that up by bringing iSCSI to a stage of relative maturity. It's time for our customers to enjoy the benefits we've brought them and for us as an industry to rest on our laurels.

Ah, but there's the rub. Storage virtualization, and its cousin, storage networks, were supposed to improve utilization of our customers' storage assets by making it possible to reconfigure and redeploy them as needs changed in the data center and across the enterprise. And they do that—all of the major vendors have delivered impressive toolsets for virtualizing storage devices and provisioning them to consumers. More forward-looking ones, like VERITAS, EMC, and others, have realized that managing heterogeneous devices as a homogeneous whole is the name of the game, and their network tools support all major storage and network components. But it turns out that that's only half the battle.

It's sure handy to be able to dismantle a 100 gigabyte striped mirrored virtual device that a Solaris server no longer needs and reconstitute it as two 25 gigabyte ones for an AIX transaction database server and four smaller striped ones for a Linux web server. And when we view the problem from a storage perspective, that's how we describe it—as a problem of reconfiguring storage resources and moving them from one server to another. But what if we looked at the problem from our user's perspective? A data center manager is much more likely to describe his or her problem as something like, "My legacy sales app that runs on Solaris is being replaced by a WebSphere app on a new AIX server, and I have to move this year's online transaction history to the new platform and find new storage for it as well. I'm also getting complaints from my CRM users that their Linux databases keep getting corrupted, and they need to be able to 'turn back the clock' for a couple of hours at any time."

Being an astute and perceptive person, our data center manager would notice that since he or she only has to keep this year's sales history online for the new AIX sales app, 150 gigabytes of physical storage is being freed up. Being up on the latest technology, our manager realizes that he or she can reconfigure this freed-up storage and deploy part of it to the new AIX server and part to the Linux servers, and use it to take hourly split mirror snapshots, which he or she will recycle every four hours. Being also a methodical person, our manager will lay out and execute a migration plan that looks something like this:

Back up the Solaris sales history for this year.

Delete the Solaris file systems and virtual devices.

Create new virtual devices and provision them to AIX and Linux.

Create file systems on AIX and restore the sales history data onto them.

Create scripts to take hourly snapshots of Linux CRM data and recycle the oldest one every four hours.

As major suppliers and "trusted advisors" to this data center manager, we should ask ourselves how we help him or her solve this problem. Our answers will depend on what we supply.

The backup vendor will say, "Well, I supply backup software that allows my customers to back up on one system and restore on another."

The disk array vendor will say, "Well, my customers can create and delete virtual devices."

The network vendor will say, "Well, my customers can redirect storage devices from any host in the SAN to any other."

The file system vendor will say, "Well, my customers can take snapshots of their data as often as they'd like."

And this, too, is true. We all do excellent jobs of storage management in our respective realms. But we're leaving the higher level problem of using information technology to achieve business goals up to our customers. Why did this data center manager have to figure all this out for him- or herself? Why does he or she have to back up and restore the data, when all he or she wants to do is "move" it from one set of disks to the same set of disks on a different platform? As an industry, we are empowering our customers with magical new capabilities. But at the same time, we're creating an enormous requirement for highly skilled administrators who can look out across a data center with hundreds of servers (not the three in our little example), continually juggle tens of thousands of variables, and make optimal storage and data management decisions. We're delivering drills and wrenches, when what our collective customers need is robots and assembly lines.

This is not to say that we've done anything bad as an industry. Indeed, if we compare the capabilities we've enabled by virtualizing storage and putting it on a network with what was available to our customers a decade ago, the difference is astounding. But the key word here is "enabled." We've made it possible for our customers to create environments that are orders of magnitude more complex than what they could have contemplated in the mid-1990s, and we've left it up to them to manage the complexity.

It's time for us as a storage industry to take a hard look at how our customers see things and try to make IT life as they see it (not as we see it) easier. Why aren't our file systems better integrated with our virtual storage so they can grow, shrink, and respond to failures appropriately? Indeed, why does every one of our platforms have a different file system format so that we're forced to copy data when all we want to do is move it from one platform to another? Why don't our mirrored virtual devices recognize that their component LUNs are in different buildings of a campus, and when they grow, they have to grow under that constraint? Why don't our application developers have APIs that let them say things like, "replicas of this database can never be more than three minutes out of date"? Why can't a virtual storage device recognize that the sales database is using 90% of available I/O bandwidth and throw more resources at the problem before it gets critical? The storage systems we deliver today collectively have the information and capabilities to automate these kinds of actions. Why aren't we doing it?

As storage developers, we've done a great job. Advanced storage technology is in some measure responsible for many things we take for granted today that didn't exist a decade ago—mobile communications, the active Internet, video on demand, reliable business-to-business transactions, and so forth. Now it's time for us to take the next step . . . to ratchet up the capabilities we deliver to our users and enable them to fully utilize the impressive array of technology we've made available to them.

Virtualization of Data

Storage Network Manager

A Fortune 500 Company in the Pacific Northwest

I consider virtualization to be multifaceted. Where I am concerned the most is the apparent lack of movement toward disk virtualization similar to EVA. I want disks to be little square things we shove into a controller on the back side, while the front-end interface allows me to

1. Group like (speed, size, technology) disks, add to pool.
2. Ungroup disks, remove from pool.
3. Leverage any RAID type LUNs drawn from the same large total pool or smaller.

A land where disk data is moved about freely and performance requirements are met by rapid data migration in the pool: This is current in some controllers, and we need it in more of them.

In the future the file system should be assembled across different LUNs with different cost and availability metrics and files are tagged/placed based on their value, security, and retention policies. It's an HSM hybrid where the storage and file system create an ecostructure together. Cheap old data is retired, and each we'll need less online storage.

I think the term virtualization has had its day. I'd like to see birth and death of a file and all the care and feeding that goes along with it through its journey on the media. It's not just disk or LUN virtualization, its data virtualization.

Benefiting from Virtualization

Gary Orenstein

Author of *IP Storage: Straight to the Core* (Addison-Wesley), which focuses on maximizing the business value of enterprise storage technology.

Recent technological developments deliver tremendous flexibility to build and architect network storage solutions. By far the most prominent trends are disk space and CPU density. We can achieve significantly larger capacities with significantly higher processing power in smaller and less–power-intensive configurations than ever before.

To be effective, aggregating drive space and processing power requires virtualization capabilities that present multiple components as a single logical pool. Whether a group of disk drives presenting a single logical unit number (LUN) or a set of clustered file servers presenting a single file space, underlying virtualization tools currently deliver on this requirement.

Carrying forward, one can envision the ability to continuously add capacity or processing power to any storage solution and then divide resources as needed. In once sense, this organic growth provides a never-ending roadmap. Grid computing often refers to this as a "scale out" architecture.

If only that were the case. Looking historically at technological constraints, an ongoing cycle exists between growing bigger and growing smarter, neither of which covers market needs alone.

An interesting parallel exists in the networking market. Ethernet has and continues to defy preconceived bandwidth limits. Over a short timeframe we've seen thousand-fold improvements in bandwidth, providing virtually unlimited capacity. At the same time, we've seen a large market for bandwidth management devices and software within local and wide area environments. No matter how bigger we make the pipes, there remains a need to be more efficient about their use.

The same effects will play out in the storage market, particularly with large, virtualized storage architectures. It is more than just a matter of more capacity or performance, but how effectively it can be used.

There are two primary steps to get us there. Facing an increasing physical number of resources, the software and hardware tools to aggregate, virtualize, and manage storage will remain critical. But the more important step will be distilling the thought processes required by information technology and business managers to use it. With more space, performance, and configuration possibilities, the bottleneck will shift toward the management time and attention required to optimize resources. This is the critical gap going forward for virtualization. New solutions will need to set constraints on the human capital required for deployment and find ways to minimize this part of the equation. Today the time for assessment, planning, implementation, maintenance, and optimization storage solutions often outweighs the benefits of deploying a new solution.

Tools restricting administrative decisions to the essentials will fulfill the promise of large virtualized network storage configurations. The greatest savings and advantages will come from delivering capacity, performance, and reliability coupled with a decision framework that minimizes management oversight. Ultimately, this will allow more users to interact with more applications that access a larger and more flexible pool of centrally managed storage.

Future Directions for Virtualization: A Foundation for the Future

Benjamin F. Kuo

Product Marketing Manager, Troika Networks

As with any technology, virtualization has gone through the usual hype cycle—where the technology is first touted for technology's sake as the "next great thing," then oversold by marketers and analysts, maligned by the early adopters when it doesn't meet their expectations, and finally finding its niche with customers who have ignored all the hype and found where the technology really fits. It looks like virtualization has finally found its niche, which is not as a standalone technology, but as an enabler to the next level of storage applications.

Customers are now finding that the benefits that virtualization provides—which include consolidation of resources, easier management of infrastructure, and simplification and centralization of storage applications—are being incorporated not only into standalone products, but integrated into solutions across a wide spectrum. Software providers who spearheaded the original push to add virtualization to Storage Area Networks have gone beyond promoting "virtualization" as a technology and instead have learned that what customers really care about: solving their pressing data storage needs. When it comes down to buying solutions, they are less concerned about the whiz bang technology of "virtualization," and more concerned about if those solutions can provide them with the ability to protect and manage their data better. Whether a product helps them manage their data center better through virtualization or any other technology, when it comes down to the bottom line, customers are only concerned about how well it helps them achieve their goals.

To a large part, you can see that companies have learned this lesson well. Instead of selling "in-band" and "out-of-band" virtualization, companies instead are pointing out how features such as snapshot, mirroring, and replication (running on top of virtualization capabilities) help the process of backing up and protecting data. Instead of debating philosophy on which virtualization technique is the "right one," companies have realized that it's the performance, features, and reliability of their solutions that determine if customers will buy their products. Companies, of course, haven't given up on using their particular technology mix as a differentiator, but the industry has matured enough that companies understand that virtualization isn't what brings customers to the table—it's the benefits that virtualization techniques bring to features running on top of it.

If you review the marketing materials and websites of companies that several years ago were on the virtualization bandwagon, instead of talk about virtualization techniques, you see focus on disk utilization, reduced backup times, better tolerance for planned and unplanned downtime, centralized management, and better management of disk storage growth.

Where does this put virtualization in the future? Clearly, virtualization technology is now becoming a mainstream, required function of nearly every component in a storage area network. It's now becoming apparent that virtualization functionality is also key to such emerging movements as information lifecycle management. Information Lifecycle Management (ILM), sometimes referred to as Data Lifecycle Management (DLM), strives to allow customers to optimize their use of storage, mostly through both policy and products that move data between different tiers of storage, depending on the value of that data and its age. ILM is expected to help companies manage their costs by putting less accessed and important data on cheaper disk and tape, instead of keeping expensive primary enterprise storage locked up with unimportant data. It's clear that one of the major enablers of information lifecycle management is the ability to move data from one storage device to another. Virtualization is a key way this can happen. In fact, there are startup companies that are designing software that moves data on a block-by-block level, making it possible to distribute difficult-to-manage data such as databases across multiple tiers of storage. Virtualization is a key enabler to making data portable enough to be moved readily in the context of the emerging concept of ILM.

Virtualization is now expected to be included as a standard part of products, whether those are based on host-based software, in a storage array, in the network as an appliance, or in an intelligent switch. Many storage array controllers have moved to, or will soon move to some level of virtualization—beyond the inherent virtualization they've always had in aggregating individual disks into RAID sets and volumes—including the ability to virtualize storage volumes across physically separate controllers. Some storage array providers have even touted the ability to also create volumes from competitive array providers—again, just another spin on basic virtualization techniques. Even the Fibre Channel switching providers are in the business of virtualization, with all of the major manufacturers saying they will include basic virtualization capability in what they are calling "intelligent switches." These intelligent switches will include either blades or ports that support the basic capabilities of virtualization, and either integrated as part of the switches or in tandem with third-party software, they will essentially provide virtualization techniques as part of a fabric. Other spins on virtualization show that it is becoming a basic functional add-on to any storage network—with specialized hardware appliances giving the ability to add virtualization to any storage network; specialized boards with acceleration of virtualization functionality; and even chips and network processors that give any hardware provider the ability to integrate storage virtualization functionality into their network switches, storage arrays, or servers.

All of this leads to one conclusion. Storage virtualization has now gone from "hot new technology" to a required piece of the storage solution puzzle. It's pretty clear that future products will simply adopt virtualization as a required part of the storage picture, and the technology will continue to play an important role in the future of storage.

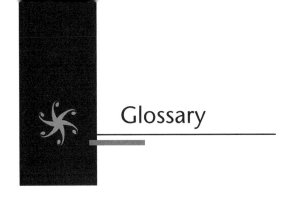

Glossary

The following glossary provides terms and definitions for both storage virtualization and general storage networking terminology. For additional storage terms, the *SNIA Dictionary* (http://www.snia.org/education/dictionary) is an excellent resource.

Access method   The means used to access a physical medium in order to transmit data.

ACL   Access Control List, a list of authorized IP addresses maintained by an IP router or switch to provide security for network access.

Actuator   In disk architecture, the component that positions the read/write heads over the disk cylinders.

Adapter card   In storage networking, an interface card installed on a server that enables access to a SAN, such as iSCSI network interface cards (NICs) and Fibre Channel host bus adapters (HBAs).

Address identifier   In Fibre Channel, a 24-bit value used to indicate the link-level address of communicating devices. In a frame header, the address.identifier indicates the source ID (S_ID) and destination ID (D_ID) of the frame.

Aggregation   For storage virtualization, the combination of multiple block address ranges into one virtual block address range via address mapping.

AH   Authentication Header, an IPSec header used to establish authorized communication between two network devices.

AIT   Advanced Intelligent Tape.

AL_PA   Arbitrated Loop Physical Address, an 8-bit value used to identify a participating device in an Arbitrated Loop.

Alternate pathing   Provisioning of two or more paths between networked devices to ensure availability in the event of a failure of a data path.

ANSI   American National Standards Institute, a governing body for technology standards in the United States.

ANSI T11.5   The ANSI technical committee whose work includes the Fabric Application Interface Standard (FAIS).

API   Application Programming Interface, an interface used by an application to request services from other applications or software components.

Appliance   A network product designed to perform a specialized task with minimal user administration. In storage virtualization, an appliance is a virtualization engine attached to a SAN.

Application   Typically, a software program running on an operating system and CPU to perform some useful purpose. In open systems, applications read and write data via SCSI I/Os processed by the operating system.

Application-aware virtualization   Virtualization intelligence that can identify specific applications and provide optimized services based on data type.

Arbitrated loop   A shared Fibre Channel transport supporting up to 126 devices and 1 fabric attachment.

Arbitration   A means for gaining orderly access to a shared loop topology.

Archive   A copy of data committed to long-term storage such as tape or optical media.

Array   A storage unit composed of disk banks and a front-end RAID controller.

Array-based virtualization   Virtualization software that runs on a storage array to provide services such as data replication and snapshots. Array-based virtualization is typically proprietary and interoperable only in homogeneous environments.

ASIC   Application Specific Integrated Circuit, an integrated circuit engineered for a specialized application.

Asynchronous   Transactions that do no require immediate acknowledgment before additional transactions are initiated.

Asynchronous data replication   A process of performing data replication between two storage arrays typically separated by distance in which writes are issued without waiting for immediate confirmation of completion by the secondary array.

ATM   Asynchronous Transfer Mode, a high-speed cell switching transport used primarily in wide area networks (WANs).

Authentication A means to verify the identity of a network device before data transmission is initiated.

Automatic data migration The transfer of block data from one virtual volume to another through use of automated virtualization instructions.

Backup Securing disk data to tape or optical media.

Backup application A software program typically installed on a dedicated server that manages tape backup processes for multiple servers.

Backup window The time required to perform nondisruptive tape backup of disk data.

Bandwidth Data transmission capacity of a link or system.

BB_Credit Buffer-to-Buffer Credit, used In Fibre Channel to determine how many frames can be sent to a recipient.

Binary A base 2 numbering system using 1s and 0s to indicate numeric value.

Bit The smallest unit of binary information used in computer systems.

BITL For FAIS, the Back I_T_L_Nexus. An identifier based on initiator, target, and LUN values to indicate a virtual storage resource.

Block A unit of contiguous data stored on disk or tape devices.

Block addressing An algorithm for identifying blocks of data stored on disk or tape by number. Also known as logical block addressing (LBA). Block address numbers are translated into physical locations on storage media, such as cylinder, head, and sector for disk media.

Block-level virtualization Logical abstraction of block address ranges through mapping and/or aggregation of blocks on one or more physical storage targets to create virtualized block resources such as virtual volumes.

Broadcast The simultaneous transmission of a message to all possible destinations on a network or network segment.

Broadcast storm Unintended flooding of a network with broadcast messages.

Bus A parallel data and control signal path typically implemented on a motherboard and used to support adapter cards and interfaces.

Byte A contiguous string of 8 binary digits, typically representing a unit of information such as an alphanumeric character.

Cable plant The complex of connectors and cabling providing physical connectivity between networked devices.

Capacity   The amount of storage available in a particular storage device or virtualized storage device.

Cascade   Connecting two or more Fibre Channel hubs or fabric switches together to increase the number of ports or extend distances.

CDB   Command Data Block. In the SCSI protocol, the CDB carries commands, status, and data between initiator and target.

Certificate   A formatted file used as a digital signature for device authentication.

Checksum   A count of the number of bits in a protocol unit that is transmitted with a packet to verify proper receipt of data.

CHS   In disk architecture, the cylinder, head, and sector parameters for locating a data block.

CIFS   Common Internet File System, a cross-platform file access protocol similar to Network File System (NFS).

CIM   Common Information Model, a management structure enabling disparate resources to be managed by a common application.

Class 1   In Fibre Channel, a connection-oriented class of service that requires acknowledgment of frame delivery.

Class 2   In Fibre Channel, a connectionless class of service that requires acknowledgment of frame delivery.

Class 3   In Fibre Channel, a connectionless class of service that requires no notification of frame delivery.

Class 4   In Fibre Channel, a class of service that defines virtual circuits via fractional bandwidth and Quality of Service parameters.

Class 6   In Fibre Channel, a class of service that provides multicast frame delivery with acknowledgment.

Class of Storage   The categorization of storage devices by performance, reliability, and cost characteristics.

CLI   Command Line Interface, typically a serial or Telnet text-driven management interface.

Client-server   An architecture that enables one computer system to receive services from another. In the SCSI protocol, the server is a client making read and write requests and the target device services those requests.

Cluster   Typically, a group of servers that run specialized software to provide automatic failover or load balancing between applications. Clustered servers monitor each other's status via heartbeat protocol.

Concatenation   The logical joining of two assets to present a single contiguous asset.   In storage virtualization, logical block address ranges from two or more storage arrays may be joined to present a virtual resource with a contiguous address range.

Connection-oriented service   Communication between two network devices that requires session establishment before data exchanges begin.

Connectionless service   Communication between two network devices that does not require session setup in advance of data exchange.

Connectivity domain   For FAIS, the set of remote ports and storage resources connected to those ports that are available from a local FAIS-enabled port.

Context switching   Concurrent processing of multiple SCSI transactions by an initiator.

Control path   The route or path between servers and a virtualization engine that carries storage metadata such as logical address mapping.

Control Path Processor (CPP)   In FAIS, a switched-based CPU that supports a virtualizaton application, the FAIS APIs, and control paths for storage metadata.

Controller   For disk arrays, the processor logic that interfaces between front-end SAN clients and back-end storage devices and provides services such as data routing, RAID, LUN creation, and error handling.

Convergence   The time required for a network to regain stability and updated routing information after a disruption.

Copy on Write (COW)   In snapshot technology, copying only data that has been modified after an initial snapshot has been taken.

Core-to-edge topology   A SAN design in which one or more large director-class switches are used to connect multiple edge switches. The edge switches provide connectivity to servers and storage; the directors provide high-performance switching between edge switches.

CoS   Class of Service, prioritization and delivery guarantees of different types of data during transport.

CPU   Central Processing Unit, typically a microprocessor in a workstation or server.

CRC   Cyclic Redundancy Check, an error detection method.

Currency   The age of data at a given point in time.

Cut-through   A switching technique that allows a routing decision to be made as soon as the destination address of a frame is received.

Cylinder   In disk architecture, a spatial location on spinning media defined by a full rotation of the disk at a given point along the disk radius. A cylinder is subdivided into sectors for data placement.

DA   Destination address.

Data   In IT, useful information in a binary format of 8-bit bytes. For SANs, data is organized in contiguous numbered blocks of a fixed quantity of bytes.

Data Lifecycle Management   The migration of data from one class of storage to another over time as the usefulness or frequency of access diminishes.

Data migration   Bulk transfer of data from one volume to another, typically between different storage arrays.

Data movement   Transfer of data from one storage system to another through data replication, data migration, serverless backup, remote mirroring, or other means.

Data path   The route or path between servers and storage systems. For in-band virtualization, the virtualizaton engine sits in the data path between storage systems and servers.

Data Path Controller (DPC)   In FAIS, the processor or CPU that executes Fast Path frame handling.

Data striping   Writing of sequential data blocks to a number of physical disks by mapping a contiguous virtual block address range to subsets of block addresses on the disks. Implemented as RAID 0, data striping improves I/O performance but provides no data protection.

Datagram   A message transmitted over a network with no link level acknowledgment of delivery.

DAFS   Direct Access File System, a protocol used for file transfer directly to system memory over Virtual Interface.

DES   Data Encryption Standard, a method of key encryption of data allowing for up to 72 quadrillion possible encryption keys.

Destination   The intended recipient of a network transmission.

Device discovery   In storage networking, any mechanism used by initiators to discover targets.

Director   A storage network switch with high port count and integrated high availability features such as redundant processors, dual power supplies, redundant fans, hot code load, and hot swap port blades.

Directory   In file systems, a structure for organizing files in a hierarchical tree. A directory may contain subdirectories and files.

Disaster recovery   Insuring business continuance by safeguarding data at a geographical distance from a primary data center.

Discovery domain   In iSNS protocol, a grouping of initiators and targets that are authorized to communicate.

Discovery domain sets Groupings of initiators and targets that have been previously defined within the same zone or domain.

Disk Typically a unit containing spinning magnetic media for persistent storage of block data.

Disk array A storage unit composed of disk banks and a front end RAID controller.

DLT Digital Linear Tape.

DMTF Distributed Management Task Force.

DNS Domain Name Server, used to resolve human-readable network domain names to IP addresses.

Dual pathing Provision of two separate data paths between networked devices. Dual pathing is typically used to provide high availability in the event of a failure of an HBA, link, switch, or storage port.

DWDM Dense Wave Division Multiplexing, use of multiple optical wavelengths within a single fiber to transmit different data streams concurrently.

E_Port An Expansion Port connecting two Fibre Channel fabric switches.

ELS Extended Link Services, status and command frames exchanged between switches or gateways.

Embedded Processing logic that provides specific services and has been integrated with other product functionality. Switch-based virtualization is an embedded service.

EMI Electromagnetic interference.

Encryption Conversion of a data payload into ciphered data by use of an encryption algorithm or key.

Enterprise A large corporation, institution, or government entity.

ESCON Enterprise Systems Connection. An IBM serial channel architecture.

Ethernet An IEEE 802.3 specification for local area network packet transmission over various media.

Exchange In Fibre Channel, an association between initiator and target for the transmission of one or more sequences of frames required for a storage operation.

Extent For files, a set of consecutive block addresses allocated for file content.

Extended Copy A SCSI command extension that enables an application to read from one storage device and write to another without server intervention. Also known as Third Party Copy.

F_Port In Fibre Channel, a switch port that provides connectivity to a Fibre Channel node (N_Port).

Fabric One or more switches in a homogeneous switched networked topology.

Fabric-based virtualization Implementing virtualization services within one or more fabric switches.

Failover The ability to sustain data access in the event of loss of a network link, host, or device.

FAIS The Fabric Application Interface Standard, formulated by the ANSI T11.5 work group.

Fast Path In FAIS, a high-performance frame processing entity, typically implemented in silicon. Once configured by the control processor, a fast path can process storage I/Os without further intervention.

Fast SCSI Parallel SCSI transmission at 10 MBps (narrow fast) or 20 MBps (wide fast) rates.

FCP Fibre Channel Protocol, the upper layer protocol for Fibre Channel serial SCSI-3 defined by ANSI T10.

FC-SW2 The ANSI standard defining Fibre Channel switch interconnect behavior.

FC SAN A storage network based on Fibre Channel hubs or switches.

FDDI Fiber Distributed Data Interface, a 100 Mbps transmission architecture for metropolitan area networks.

Fibre Channel An ANSI standard for serial gigabit transport, typically used for serial SCSI-3 upper layer protocol support.

FICON Fibre Connect. An IBM serial channel architecture for moving mainframe-generated data over Fibre Channel protocols.

File A data object composed of an order set of data bytes stored on disk or tape and identified by a symbolic name, read/write permissions, and other attributes.

File server A dedicated server or NAS device that is connected to storage and responds to client requests for file retrieval, creation, or deletion.

File locking Restricting updates to a file's contents to only one user at a time.

File sharing Enabling multiple users or applications to access a file's content concurrently. To avoid file corruption, file sharing implies file locking capabilities.

File system A hierarchical structure for the organization of directories and files, typically organized as a tree structure from the main or root directory.

File system virtualization The abstraction of a file system into a shared hierarchy between multiple servers, typically by use of a file system metadata server.

FITL For FAIS, the Front I_T_L_Nexus. An identifier based on initiator, target and LUN values to indicate a virtual association between an initiator and a virtual resource.

Fixed Block Architecture FBA, the organization of disk storage space as linear address spaces of fixed-size blocks as required by the SCSI protocol.

F_Port A port on a Fibre Channel switch that supports an N_Port.

FLOGI Fabric Login, a process by which a node establishes a logical connection to a fabric switch.

FL_Port A port on a Fibre Channel switch that supports Arbitrated Loop devices.

Flow control A mechanism for pacing traffic between source and destination over the network.

Full-duplex Concurrent transmission and reception of data on a link.

Frame A data unit composed of a start-of-frame delimiter, header, data payload, CRC, and end-of-frame delimiter.

FSPF Fabric Shortest Path First, a routing protocol for Fibre Channel fabrics; a subset of the IP Open Shortest Path First protocol.

G_Port A port on a Fibre Channel switch that supports either F_Port or E_Port functionality.

GBE Gigabit Ethernet, sometimes abbreviated to GE.

GBIC Gigabit Interface Converter, a removable transceiver module for Fibre Channel and Gigabit Ethernet physical layer transport.

Gbps Gigabits per second.

Geometry In disk architecture, the unique design of cylinders, heads, and sectors for storing block data. Proprietary disk geometries are masked by the presentation of disk storage as consecutive data block addresses.

Gigabit For Fibre Channel, 1,062,500,000 bits per second; for Gigabit Ethernet, 1,250,000,000 bits per second.

Gigabit Ethernet The IEEE 802.3z standard for Ethernet over a switched serial gigabit transport.

GUI Graphical User Interface, typically a graphical menu system for device management and configuration.

Hard zoning   Segregation of SAN devices based on port attachment.

Hardware Abstraction Layer (HAL)   A software layer that abstracts a physical hardware device from the device driver software.

HBA   Host Bus Adapter, an interface between a server or workstation bus and the Fibre Channel network.

Head   In disk architecture, the component that reads and writes bits of data to spinning magnetic media. In network-attached storage, a processing unit that services file requests (NAS head) using network file protocols.

Header   Leading bytes of addressing and parameter information attached to a packet payload.

Heartbeat protocol   A protocol that provides status messages, typically between servers in a cluster.

Heterogeneous   In storage networking, use of products from multiple vendors.

High availability   To provide continuous access to data. High availability in SANs is implemented with server clustering, dual pathing, director-class switches, hot code load, SAN routing, RAID, and advanced self-healing diagnostics for storage arrays.

HIPPI   High Performance Parallel Interface.

Homogeneous   In storage networking, use of products from a single vendor.

Host   In networking, any end device attached to the network. In storage networking, a server or workstation attached to the SAN.

Host-based virtualization   Software running on each server that virtualizes the appearance of physical storage assets. Volume management is host-based virtualization.

Hot code load   The ability to upgrade firmware on a network device without disrupting ongoing operations.

HSM   Hierarchical Storage Management, a policy-based mechanism for migrating storage data between classes of storage.

HTML   HyperText Markup Language.

HTTP   HyperText Transfer Protocol.

Hub   In Fibre Channel, a wiring concentrator that collapses a loop topology into a physical star topology.

HVD   High Voltage Differential, a SCSI parallel cable interface.

I/O   Input/Output, an operation that transfers data to or from a computer.

IETF   Internet Engineering Task Force, the standards body responsible for IP-related standards.

iFCP Internet Fibre Channel Protocol. Fibre Channel Layer 4 FCP over TCP/IP.

In-band Transmission of management protocol over the network transport.

In-band virtualization A virtualization technique that positions the virtualization engine in the data path. For servers, the in-band virtualizer appears as a storage target.

Initiator Typically a server or workstation on a storage network that initiates transactions to disk or tape targets.

Intelligent switch A network switch providing both switching services and enhanced services such as transport optimization, frame content processing, security, or virtualization services.

Interswitch link Connection between two network switches. In Fibre Channel, E_Ports provide interswitch links.

IP Internet Protocol, the most widely used layer 3 network protocol.

IPS Working Group The standards workgroup within the IETF currently developing IP storage protocol standards.

IP SAN A storage network based on IP switches and routers with native IP, Fibre Channel, or SCSI end devices.

IPSec IP Security, an architecture for device authentication and data encryption over IP networks.

IP storage Block data transfer using serial SCSI-3 over an IP network.

iSCSI Internet SCSI, serial SCSI-3 block data transport over TCP/IP.

iSCSI Consortium A multivendor organization established by the University of New Hampshire for standards compliance testing.

iSNS Internet Storage Name Server, a discovery and management protocol for IP storage networks.

ISO International Standards Organization.

ISP Internet Service Provider.

ISV Independent Software Vendor.

IT Information Technology. An umbrella term that encompasses applications, data processing, computer platforms, operating systems, networking, storage, and data management.

JBOD Just A Bunch of Disks, typically configured as a Fibre Channel Arbitrated Loop segment in a single chassis.

KB Kilobyte. For storage networking, 1000 data bytes.

LAN   Local Area Network, a network linking multiple devices in a single geographical location.

LAN-free backup   Tape backup operations in which storage data traverses a SAN instead of the local area network.

Latency   The time interval between initiating and completing a transaction. For wide area transport, latency between source and destination is primarily due to speed of light propagation delay.

LBA   See Logical Block Address.

LBA mapping   Mapping logical block addresses to virtual block addresses to create larger virtual volumes or subdivide a physical volume into smaller virtual volumes.

LDAP   Lightweight Directory Access Protocol, a protocol used for locating resources or devices on the network.

Link   The transmission connection between two devices on a network. A link may be electrical (copper), optical, or wireless.

Link state protocol   A routing protocol that calculates optimum paths through the network based on number of hops (routers), link bandwidth, and current traffic loads between routers.

LIP   Loop Initialization Primitive; used to initiate a procedure that results in unique addressing for all nodes, to indicate a loop failure, or to reset a specific node.

LLC   Logical Link Control, a data link sublayer that interfaces between media access control and upper layer network protocols.

Load balancing   Sharing of a common task between multiple networked devices.

Loop   Arbitrated Loop, a shared Fibre Channel gigabit topology.

Loop Port State Machine   Logic that monitors and performs the tasks required for initialization and access to the loop.

Logical block   A block of data stored on disk or tape that is identified by a logical block number.

Logical Block Address (LBA)   The address of a logical block on disk or tape used by the SCSI protocol to write or read data.

Logical Block Address Range   A consecutive range of logical block addresses in a disk asset.

Logical Unit (LU)   The entity within a storage target that executes SCSI I/O commands.

LUN   Logical Unit Number, a SCSI identifier for a logical unit within a storage target.

LUN mapping   A technique for assigning a virtual LUN number to a real one.

LUN masking   A mechanism for making only designated LUNs visible to an initiator.

LVD   Low Voltage Differential, a SCSI parallel cable interface.

MAC   Media Access Control.

MAID   Massive Array of Idle Disks, leveraging low-cost disks as a replacement for tape backup.

MAN   Metropolitan Area Network, typically with a circumference of less than 100 km.

Mapping   Conversion between two data addressing spaces, typically through an algorithm. High-performance mapping between logical block addresses and virtual block addresses is an essential activity for storage virtualization.

Mapping boundary   The first and last blocks within a virtualized block address range.

Mb   Megabits. For storage, one million (10^6) data bits.

MB   Megabyte. For storage, one million (10^6)bytes.

MBps   Megabytes per second.

Mbps   Megabits per second.

Media   For storage, the physical material used for data storage, typically magnetic disk, tape, or optical.

Metadata   Data that describes data. In file systems, file metadata includes file name, time of creation/modification, read/write permissions, and lists of block addresses at which the file's data is stored. For virtualization, storage metadata includes the mapping tables that link virtual block addresses to logical block addresses of physical disks.

Metadata server   A dedicated processor that maintains and services block address translation tables.

MIA   Media Interface Adapter; a device that converts optical signaling to electrical.

MIB   Management Information Base; an SNMP structure for device management.

Migration   The process of transferring storage data from one storage device to another, typically from one class of storage to another for data lifecycle management.

Mirror   An exact copy of disk data written in real time to a secondary disk or array.

Multicast   A network transmission from a single source to multiple destinations concurrently.

Multipath   Provisioning multiple network connections between initiators and targets within the SAN.

Multipath I/O   Directing SCSI I/O requests to a storage target over two or more access paths.

N_Port   A Fibre Channel node port in a point-to-point or node to fabric connection.

NAS   Network-Attached Storage, a disk array connected to a controller that provides file access over a LAN transport.

NCITS   National Committee for Information Technology Standards.

NDMP   Network Data Management Protocol, a protocol for performing tape backups without consuming server resources.

Network   A complex of nodes or end devices connected by communication paths.

Network-based storage virtualization   Virtualization services provided by appliances attached to a SAN or by virtualization engines embedded within fabric switches.

NFS   Network File System, a cross-platform file access protocol.

NIC   Network Interface Card.

NL_Port   Node Loop Port; a port that support Arbitrated Loop protocol.

NOC   Network Operations Center, an IP network monitoring and management facility.

Node   A Fibre Channel entity that supports one or more ports.

Node_Name   A unique 64-bit identifier assigned to a Fibre Channel Node.

NVRAM   Nonvolatile random access memory.

OLTP   Online Transaction Processing.

Open system   A system whose operations and infrastructure are based on common standards.

OS   Operating system.

OSI   Open Systems Interconnection.

OSI reference model   A 7-layer abstraction of common data networking functions.

Out-of-band   Transmission of management protocol outside of the Fibre Channel network, typically over Ethernet.

Packet   A unit of data transported over a network.

Parallel   The simultaneous transmission of multiple data bits over multiple lines in a single cable plant.

Parity RAID   Most commonly, RAID 5 in which parity is calculated on block data in a data stripe and written to disk for the reconstruction of data in the event of a disk failure.

Partition   The subdivision of the total capacity of a physical or virtual disk into consecutively numbered block address ranges.

Path   The route between one networked device and another. In a storage network, the path between a server and a storage device may pass through one or more fabric switches.

PCI   Peripheral Component Interconnect, an interface specification for a computer bus providing 66 MHz performance.

PCI-X   Peripheral Component Interconnect Extended, an interface specification for a computer bus providing 133 MHz performance.

Persistent data   Data that has been written to nonvolatile media such as disk or tape. Data in memory is not persistent since a power outage will result in data loss.

PKI   Public Key Infrastructure, a security mechanism for authentication and data encryption.

PLOGI   In Fibre Channel, a port-to-port login process by which initiators establish sessions with targets.

Point in time copy   Creation of a copy of block data at a specific point in time, typically used to restore data access in the event of later data corruption. Also known as snapshot.

Point-to-point   A dedicated network connection between two devices.

Policy   A set of rules for the behavior of a device or process under given conditions.

Policy-based virtualization   The use of policies to automate virtualization services for disparate applications and conditions.

Port   A physical entity that connects a node to the network.

Port_Name   In Fibre Channel, a unique 64-bit identifier assigned to a Fibre Channel port.

Port number   In TCP and UDP, a 16-bit integer used by the transport layer to associate transactions with upper layer applications.

PPRC   Peer-to-Peer Remote Copy. Data replication software for IBM Shark storage systems.

Private loop   A free-standing arbitrated loop with no fabric attachment.

Private loop device   An arbitrated loop device that does not support fabric login.

Proprietary   Nonstandard processes or protocols specific to an individual vendor.

Public loop   An arbitrated loop attached to a fabric switch.

Public loop device   An arbitrated loop device that supports fabric login and services.

QoS   Quality of Service, frame delivery preference based on acknowledgment, prioritization, and bandwidth parameters.

Quiesce   To suspend operation of an application or process, typically to capture or copy a static state of data at a given time.

RAID   Redundant Array of Independent Disks, designed to provide data reconstruction in the event of disk failure.

RAID-0   Striping of data across multiple physical disks to enhance performance. RAID-0 provides no data protection.

RAID 0+1   Combining striping and mirroring for both performance and data redundancy. Also known as RAID 1+0.

RAID-1   Mirroring of data, typically between separate disk arrays.

RAID-5   Striping of data across multiple drives with parity.

RAIL   Redundant Array of Independent Libraries.

RAIT   Redundant Array of Independent Tape devices.

RAS   Reliability, availability, and serviceability.

Read   To retrieve data from disk or tape media.

Record   In database applications, a structured unit of data items.

Recovery   Restoration of data operations following a disruption.

Redundancy   Provision multiple components, devices, or paths to provide high availability.

Remote data replication   Typically disk-to-disk data replication over distance by synchronous or asynchronous means. Often used for disaster recovery.

RFC   Request for Comments, standards document used by the IETF as a vehicle for consensus on standards and further standards development.

RPO   Recovery point objective. The currency of data required to resume operations following a failure. For high-availability applications, the RPO is the very last transaction that occurred before an outage.

RSCN   Registered State Change Notification, a switch function that allows notification to registered nodes if a change occurs to other, specified nodes.

RTO   Recovery Time Objective. The length of time following a failure that data operations should be restored. For some businesses, the RTO may be an hour or more; for other businesses, the RTO may be zero and require immediate restoration of operations.

SA   Source Address.

SAM-2   The SCSI Architectural Model.

SAN   Storage Area Network; a network linking servers or workstations to disk arrays, tape backup subsystems, and other devices, typically over gigabit transports such as Fibre Channel or Gigabit Ethernet using serial block protocols.

SAN island   A standalone storage network installation.

SAN router   A storage network switch used to connect separate SANs for storage transactions without building a common fabric.

SAS   Serial-attached SCSI.

SATA   Serial ATA.

Scalability   The ability to support growth of a system or network over time.

Schema   A collection of structured information or data models.

SCN   State change notification, a mechanism for proactively alerting initiators to changes in the availability of storage targets.

SCSI   Small Computer Systems Interface, both a protocol for transmitting large blocks of data and a parallel bus architecture.

SCSI bus   A parallel bus that supports the simultaneous transmission of bits for SCSI I/O.

SCSI-3   A SCSI standard that defines transmission of SCSI protocol over serial links.

Sector   In disk architecture, a fixed length area subdivided from a disk cylinder and head position. A sector on the disk geometry typically represents a single fixed-size data block.

Segmentation   The division of data blocks into sequential frames or packets for transmission over a network.

Serial   The transmission of data bits in sequential order over a single line.

Server   A computer that processes end-user requests for data and/or applications.

Serverless backup   Use of Third Party Copy (Extended Copy) to perform tape backup without requiring backup data to pass through a server.

Single mode   A fiber optic cabling specification that provides up to 10 km distance between devices.

Skew   The time frame within which all bits in a parallel transmission must be received.

SLA   Service Level Agreement,   quality of service guarantees between a provider and client.

SLP   Service Locator Protocol, a protocol for querying lists of network resources.

SNIA   Storage Networking Industry Association.

Snapshot   A point-in-time copy of block data. Snapshots are used to restore data access to a known good point in time if data corruption subsequently occurs or to preserve an image of data for non-disruptive tape backup.

SNMP   Simple Network Management Protocol, a network management protocol designed to run over TCP/IP routed networks.

SNS   Simple Name Server, a service provided by a fabric switch that simplifies discovery of devices.

SNW   Storage Network World, storage networking conferences sponsored by the Storage Networking Industry Association and Computerworld.

Soft Zoning   Segregation of SAN devices based on World Wide Name or network address.

Solid state disk   A disk controller that uses random-access memory for storage. Also known as RAM disk.

SONET   Synchronous Optical Network.

Source   The origin of a network transmission.

SRDF   Symmetrix Remote Data Facility, EMC's Symmetrix disk-to-disk data replication application used primarily for disaster recovery.

SRM   Storage resource management; management of disk volumes and file resources.

SSA   Serial storage architecture, a gigabit serial storage transport superceded by Fibre Channel.

Storage   Any device used to store data; typically, magnetic disk media or tape.

Storage application   Application or utility for storage data movement, protection or virtualization, e.g., tape backup applications.

Storage NIC   A network interface card with optimized logic for TCP and serial SCSI-3 processing.

Storage pool   The virtualization of multiple physical storage systems into a common resource that can be sized and allocated to servers.

Storage system Typically, a RAID disk array or tape library with a front-end processor dedicated to data recording and retrieval.

Storage virtualization A broad category of logical abstraction mechanisms that mask the unique geometry and complexity of individual storage assets. Storage virtualization includes virtualization of disks, disk arrays, tape systems, files, and file systems.

Store-and-forward A switching technique that requires buffering an entire frame before a routing decision is made.

Striping A RAID technique for writing a single stream of data to multiple disks on block-by-block basis.

Switch A device providing full bandwidth per port and high-speed routing of data via link level or network addressing.

Synchronous Sequential operations that require acknowledgment of completion before another transaction is issued.

Synchronous data replication Typically, for disk-to-disk data replication, the execution of data writes from one array to another with acknowledgment per write.

Tape subsystem A tape backup device, typically a tape library with multiple tape drives in a single enclosure.

Tape virtualization Making multiple tape systems appear as a single tape resource, or a large tape system appear as multiple tape systems.

Target Typically a disk array or tape subsystem on a storage network. A storage virtualizer may mimic the behavior of a storage target to present virtualized LUNs to servers.

TByte Terabyte. A billion (10^{12}) data bytes.

TCO Total cost of ownership.

TCP/IP Transmission Control Protocol over Internet Protocol.

TCP connection A session established between two network devices to insure reliable data exchange.

Terabyte A measure of storage capacity equivalent to a thousand billion bytes of data.

Third-Party Copy A SCSI command extension that enables an application to read from one storage device and write to another without server intervention. Also known as Extended Copy.

TOE TCP off-load engine, typically embedded on a network interface card for processing the TCP protocol stack.

Topology The physical or logical arrangement of devices in a networked configuration.

TPC Third-Party Copy; a protocol for performing tape backups without consuming server resources.

Transaction In storage networks, an exchange between an initiator and target such as a read or write operation.

Transceiver A device that converts one form of signaling to another for both transmission and reception; in fiber optics, conversion from optical to electrical.

TrueCopy Synchronous and asynchronous data replication software for Hitachi Data System storage arrays.

Trunking For storage networks, aggregation of multiple interswitch links to provide failover or load balancing within the fabric.

Tunneling Encapsulation of entire frames of a protocol for transport through an IP network.

Ultra SCSI Parallel SCSI at 20 MBps.

Ultra2 SCSI Parallel SCSI at 40 MBps.

Ultra3 SCSI Parallel SCSI at 80 MBps.

UNH University of New Hampshire, organizer of the iSCSI Consortium for protocol standards compliance testing.

Upper layer application Typically the business application running on workstations or servers.

Upper layer protocol The protocol running on top of the layer 2 (link layer) network. IP is an upper layer protocol for Ethernet; Fibre Channel Protocol is an upper layer protocol for the Fibre Channel link layer.

User A human being chained to a computer.

User data Application data generated under the direction of a user.

VAR Value-Added Reseller.

Vaulting Archiving tape backups, typically via remote tape backup over a WAN.

VBA Virtual block address.

VDEV In FAIS, a virtual device. A VDEV may be composed of other VDEVs or logical block address ranges from back-end storage devices (BITL sets).

Vendor-specific Nonstandard features of an individual vendor's product.

VIOPs Virtual I/Os per second.

Virtual Block Address (VBA) A fabricated block address or address range presented to the server that maps to a logical block address or address range on physical storage.

Virtual disk   A set of disk blocks presented to the operating system as a range of consecutively numbered logical blocks with disk-like storage and SCSI I/O semantics.

Virtualization   Technology for creating a logical abstraction of physical assets.

Virtualization engine   A processor that performs virtual block address to logical block address mapping and provides services such as storage pooling, replication and snapshots.

Virtualization entity   A software component that performs block address mapping and executes services such as replication or snapshots. The virtualization entity may reside in a host, storage device, switch or appliance.

Virtualization-aware applications   Applications that can inform a virtualization entity of its specific storage requirements.

Volume   A virtual block storage device that mimics the behavior of a physical disk asset.

Volume management   Typically, host-based software used to aggregate or subdivide physical storage assets into virtual volumes.

WAN   Wide Area Network, a network linking geographically remote sites.

WBEM   Web-based enterprise management.

Wide SCSI   A SCSI parallel cable interface with 16 data lines.

WMD   Weapons of Mass Destruction.

Word   Typically, 4 contiguous bytes processed as a single instruction by a computer processor.

World-Wide Name   A registered, unique 64-bit identifier assigned to Nodes and Ports.

Write   To record data on disk or tape media.

Write sequencing   For data replication, ensuring that the order in which multiple writes are issued is maintained from source to destination to guarantee data integrity.

WWUI   World Wide Unique Identifier, an identifier used by iSCSI comparable to a Fibre Channel World Wide Name.

XML   Extensible Markup Language.

XMAP   For FAIS, an object that keeps track of regions within a virtual device (VDEV).

Zoning   A function provided by fabric switches that allows segregation of nodes by physical port or World Wide Name.

Bibliography

Bach, Maurice J. *The Design of the Unix Operating System.* Englewood Cliffs, NJ: Prentice Hall, 1986.

Barker, Richard and Massiglia, Paul. *Storage Area Network Essentials.* New York: John Wiley & Sons, 2001.

Benner, Alan F. *Fibre Channel.* New York: McGraw-Hill, 1996.

Benner, Alan F. *Fibre Channel for SANs.* New York: McGraw-Hill, 2001.

Breyer, Robert and Sean Riley. *Switched, Fast, and Gigabit Ethernet.* Indianapolis, IN: Macmillan, 1999.

Clark, Tom. *Designing Storage Area Networks: A Practical Reference for Implementing Fibre Channel SANs.* Reading, MA: Addison-Wesley, 1998. Also in Chinese translation, Pearson, 2003, ISBN 7-5083-1319-3, and in Japanese translation, Nanosoft, 2000, ISBN 89471-272-5.

Clark, Tom. *IP SANs, A Guide to iSCSI, iFCP and FCIP Protocols for Storage Area Networks.* Reading, MA: Addison-Wesley, 2001. Also in Chinese translation, Pearson, 2003, ISBN 7-5083-1510-3, and in Japanese translation, Soft Bank, 2002, ISBN 4-7973-2185-7.

Clark, Tom. *Designing Storage Area Networks Second Edition: A Practical Reference for Implementing Fibre Channel and IP SANs.* Reading, MA: Addison-Wesley, 2003.

Cunningham, David and William Lane. *Gigabit Ethernet Networking.* Indianapolis, IN: Macmillan, 1999.

Davie, Bruce et al. *Switching in IP Networks.* San Francisco: Morgan Kaufmann, 1998.

Dons, Bram. *Opslagnetwerken, DAS, SAN en NAS.* The Netherlands: Academic Service, 2003.

Farley, Marc. *Building Storage Networks*. Berkeley, CA: Osborne, 2000.

Field, Gary et al. *The Book of SCSI*. San Francisco: No Starch Press, 1999.

Hufferd, John. *iSCSI: The Universal Storage Connection*. Reading, MA: Addison-Wesley, 2002.

Kembel, Robert W. *The Fibre Channel Consultant: Arbitrated Loop*. Tucson, AZ: Northwest Learning Associates, 1997.

Kembel, Robert W. *The Fibre Channel Consultant: A Comprehensive Introduction*. Tucson, AZ: Northwest Learning Associates, 1998.

Kembel, Robert W. *The Fibre Channel Consultant: Fibre Channel Switched Fabric*. Tucson, AZ: Northwest Learning Associates, 2001.

Massiglia, Paul. *Disk Storage Management for Windows Servers*. Mountain View, CA: VERITAS, 2001.

Massiglia, Paul. *Virtual Storage Redefined*. Mountain View, CA: VERITAS, 2003.

Massiglia, Paul. *Highly Available Storage for Windows Servers*. New York: John Wiley & Sons, 2001.

Naik, Dilip. *Inside Windows Storage*. Reading, MA: Addison-Wesley, 2004.

Orenstein, Gary. *IP Storage Networking, Straight to the Core*. Reading, MA: Addison-Wesley, 2003.

Perlman, Radia. *Interconnections* (2nd ed.). Reading, MA: Addison-Wesley, 2000.

Preston, Curtis. *Using SANs and NAS*. Sebastopol, CA: O'Reilly and Associates, 2002.

Schulz, Greg. *Resilient Storage Networks*. Burlington, MA: Elsevier Digital Press, 2004.

Seifert, Rich. *Gigabit Ethernet*. Reading, MA: Addison-Wesley, 1999.

Simitci, Huseyin. *Storage Networking Performance Analysis*. Indianapolis, IN: John Wiley & Sons, 2003.

Stai, Jeffrey D. *The Fibre Channel Bench Reference*. Saratoga, CA: ENDL Publications, 1996.

Stevens, W. Richard. *TCP/IP Illustrated in Three Volumes*. Reading, MA: Addison-Wesley, 2000.

Thornburgh, Ralph. *Fibre Channel for Mass Storage*. Upper Saddle River, NJ: Prentice Hall, 1999.

Toigo, Jon William. *Disaster Recovery Planning.* Upper Saddle River, NJ: Prentice Hall, 2002.

Toigo, Jon William. *The Essential Guide to Application Service Providers.* Upper Saddle River, NJ: Prentice Hall, 2001.

Toigo, Jon William. *The Holy Grail of Data Storage Management.* Upper Saddle River, NJ: Prentice Hall, 1999.

Troppens, Ulf and Rainer Erkens. *Speichernetze, Grundlagen und Einsatz von Fibre Channel SAN, NAS, iSCSI und InfiniBand.* Heidelberg, Germany: dpunkt.verlag GmbH, 2003.

Index

Also Available from Addison-Wesley and Tom Clark

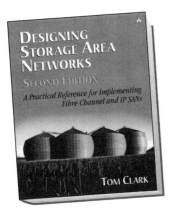

Designing Storage Area Networks, Second Edition
A Practical Reference for Implementing Fibre Channel and IP SANs
BY TOM CLARK

Written for network developers, IT consultants, administrators, and managers, this updated and greatly expanded edition of the best-selling *Designing Storage Area Networks* goes far beyond a straight description of technical specifications and standards. The text offers practical guidelines for using diverse SAN technologies to solve existing networking problems in large-scale corporate networks. With this book you will learn how the technologies work and how to organize their components into an effective, scalable design. In doing so, you will discover today's best methods for managing storage area networks, including new troubleshooting techniques.

ISBN 0-321-13650-0, © 2003, 592 pages

IP SANs
A Guide to iSCSI, iFCP, and FCIP Protocols for Storage Area Networks
BY TOM CLARK

IP storage and networking have traditionally resided in two distinct worlds. Networking professionals from an Internet Protocol (IP) internetworking background are usually not familiar with storage issues, and storage administrators may be unfamiliar with IP internetworking. With IP storage networking, network professionals dealing with storage area networks (SANs) now have an integrated option for improved data storage. IP SANs explains these new IP technologies that enable SANs to keep up with today's networking needs, detailing the various storage solutions that are created when both disciplines are combined.

ISBN 0-201-75277-8, © 2001, 320 pages

 Visit us online for more books and more information, and to read sample chapters:
http://www.awprofessional.com

Wouldn't it be great

if the world's leading technical
publishers joined forces to deliver
their best tech books in a common
digital reference platform?

They have. Introducing
InformIT Online Books
powered by Safari.

■ **Specific answers to specific questions.**
InformIT Online Books' powerful search engine gives you
relevance-ranked results in a matter of seconds.

■ **Immediate results.**
With InformIT Online Books, you can select the book
you want and view the chapter or section you need
immediately.

■ **Cut, paste and annotate.**
Paste code to save time and eliminate typographical
errors. Make notes on the material you find useful and
choose whether or not to share them with your work
group.

■ **Customized for your enterprise.**
Customize a library for you, your department or your entire
organization. You only pay for what you need.

Get your first 14 days FREE!
For a limited time, InformIT Online Books is offering
its members a 10 book subscription risk-free for
14 days. Visit **http://www.informit.com/online-**
books for details.

informit.com/onlinebooks